S0-FER-406

VICTORIA DUERSTOCK

THE STORY OF *good*

END GAME Press

The Story of Good

Copyright © 2022 by Victoria Duerstock
All rights reserved.

No part of this work may be reproduced or transmitted in any form or by any means, electronic or mechanical, including photocopying and recording, or by any information storage or retrieval system, except as may be expressly permitted by the 1976 Copyright Act or in writing from the publisher. Requests for permission can emailed to info@endgamepress.com.

End Game Press books may be purchased in bulk at special discounts for sales promotion, corporate gifts, ministry, fund-raising, or educational purposes. Special editions can also be created to specifications. For details, contact Special Sales Dept., End Game Press, P.O. Box 206, Nesbit, MS 38651 or info@endgamepress.com.

Visit our website at www.endgamepress.com

Library of Congress Control Number: 2022932802
ISBN: 978-1-63797-021-8
eBook ISBN: 978-1-63797-022-5

Cover Design by Megan Phillips, Megan Phillips Design
Interior design by Monica Thomas & Marisa Jackson for TLC Book Design, TLCBookDesign.com

Printed in India
TPL
10 9 8 7 6 5 4 3 2 1

THE STORY OF GOOD

is dedicated to my family by blood and by marriage who serve selflessly in various capacities all over the nation and to all the amazing, ordinary people in the world today that are doing good.

come with me,

where dreams
are born,

and time is

never planned.

-Peter Pan

TABLE OF CONTENTS

ABLE	1
Anchal	7
Bel Kai	13
Bella Tunno	19
CADDIS	25
Crave Candles Co	31
dŌSA Naturals	37
FarmHouse Fresh	43
Generous Coffee	49
Happiness Project	55
KaAn'S Designs	61
MudLOVE	67
Musee	73
New Hope Girls	79
Pura Vida	85
Raggidy Edges	91
Ranger Station	97
Sackcloth & Ashes	103
Spoonful of Imagination	109
Two Blind Brothers	115
Utopian Coffee	121
Vera Bradley	127
Village Thrive	133
Xocolatl	139
Behind the Story	145
From the Author	157
Bibliography	159
More Reading	161

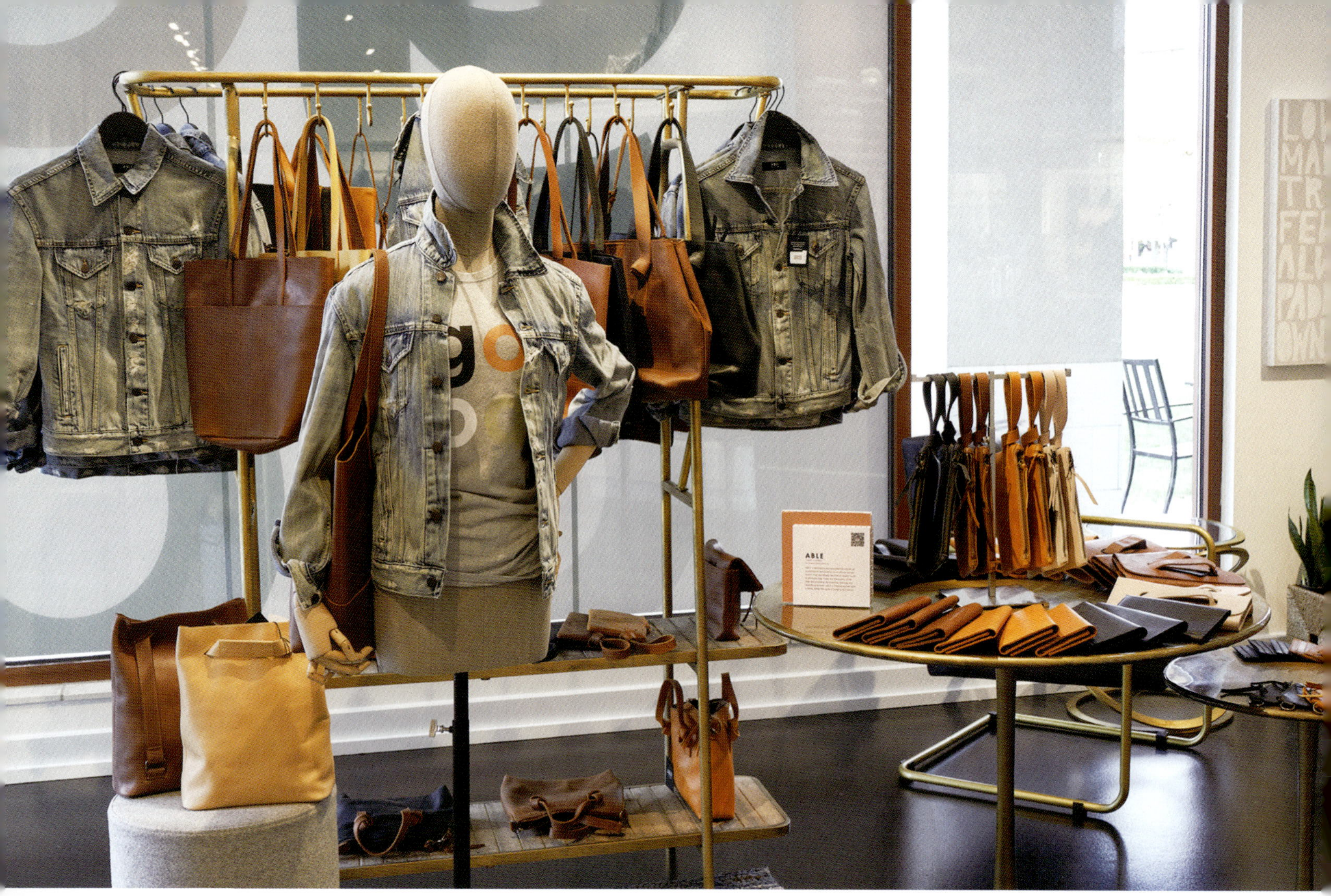
ABLE

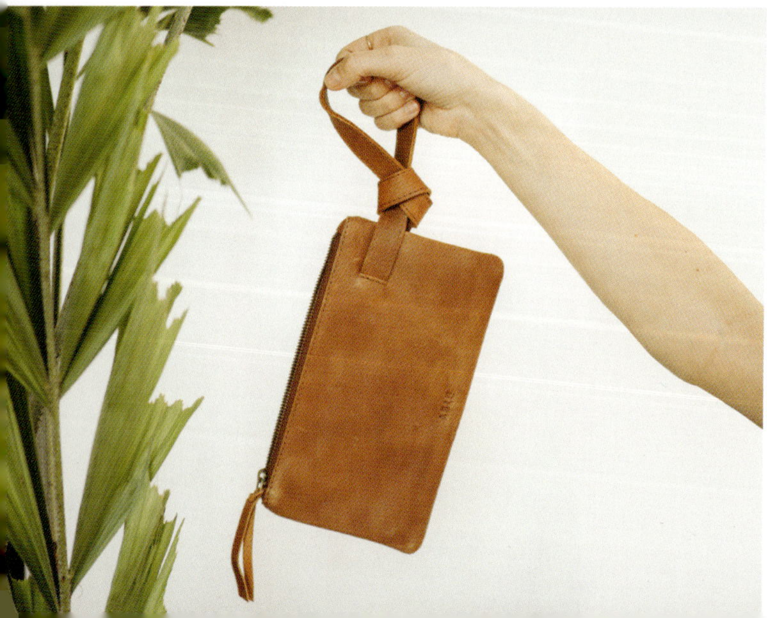

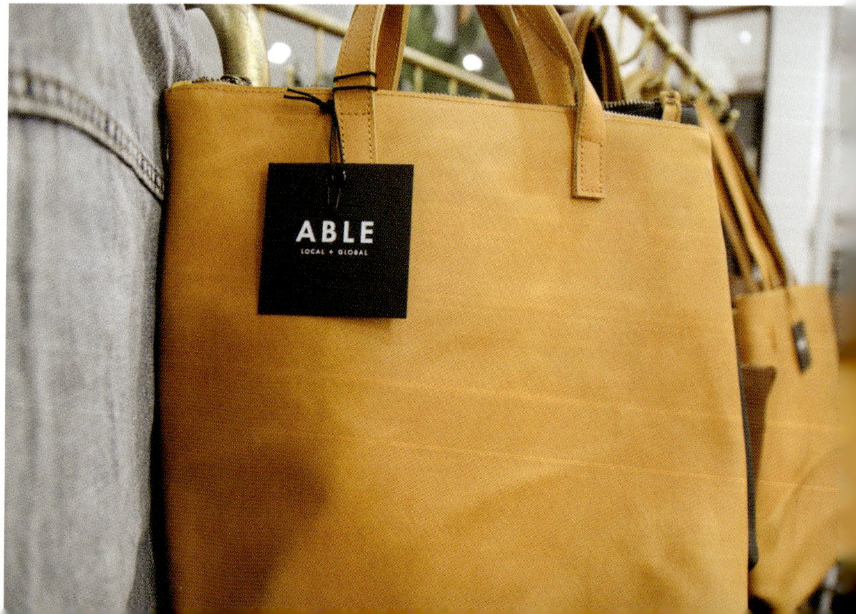
ABLE
LOCAL + GLOBAL

SUSTAINABLE & ETHICAL PRODUCTION — good — WOMEN'S EMPOWERMENT

ABLE

Forged over time, a vision for purpose-driven business propels some leaders forward. Other times it's simply a response in the moment to seeing someone in need and wanting to help. The latter is the case with ethical fashion brand ABLE. No vision board or mission statements in sight, Barrett Ward, founder of ABLE, describes the beginnings of a future movement as simply responding to the need he saw while living in Ethiopia with his wife. He recognized that the people, specifically the women, didn't need charity, rather they needed an opportunity. Since those early days, Ward has put his intentions front and center. Their mission is simple—provide opportunities for women, and challenge the culture of the fashion industry today.

ABLE is an ethical fashion brand that employs and empowers women specifically as a means to end poverty. Ward knows that to impact the fashion industry you need the power of consumer demand, which means that the products ABLE produces must be first class. And impact he will, because he also values the quality of life for the artisans and workers who design and create the products. Being committed to the goal of providing a fair living wage to help break the endless cycles of poverty, they also invest in the women who work for them by providing training and education.

A need described, and a solution provided.

Like many of the other brands in this book, the mission and courage to make an impact launched with a single purpose yet expanded exponentially over time. In this case, it started with scarves.

The need to offer dignified, sustainable jobs that would allow women to provide for themselves and

1

so for women even more so as they are the nurturers of their communities.

Women comprise most of the staff at ABLE—ninety-nine percent! This includes the highest levels of the company. Ward realized they were dealing with a global problem and by leveraging fashion in a new way they could scale their impact with job creation. The cycle of poverty in many Third World countries often continues because women often hold the lowest paying and least secure jobs, and many put all they do earn into caring for their families. The founders of ABLE realized that when a woman is economically empowered, her children their families, prompted the new business venture. Because the ladies chose scarves, this was the business that Ward helped launch.

Training women to make scarves after leaving the commercial sex industry became the initial means that ABLE used to provide jobs and an opportunity to earn a living in a new way. The success of the solution was selling over four thousand scarves in two months! At that point, they recognized a practical truth. People understood that if you're serious about solutions to poverty, you must create jobs, and to do

> "It's important to think good, speak good, and do good. If we want to see positive change in the world, then we need to connect to goodness. I try in everything I do, both in business and philanthropy, to make a positive change and do that by doing good."
>
> —SHARI ARISON, *best-selling author, businesswoman, and philanthropist*

and community thrive. This makes women a critical part of the important mission to eradicate poverty. To this end, ABLE maintains a commitment to valuing women in not only the way they are treated, but also by encouraging their partners to provide fair, livable wages.

They have found that creating these jobs and making beautiful products go hand in hand. Because of this, ABLE has grown from hand-woven scarves to a complete lifestyle brand, encompassing many categories including leather bags, clothes, shoes, and jewelry. They design for the staples in the wardrobe with a nod toward trends.

Because the fashion industry is one of the largest employers of women worldwide, and because so many of these employees don't make a fair living wage, this was an area in which ABLE could make an enormous impact. One initiative ABLE launched to ensure their goal of offering living wages to their workers was to give back margin points to a factory they worked with enabling the factory to earn more profit if they treated their employees fairly.

ABLE believes that if the everyday customer knew with absolute transparency what ABLE has learned to be true about the fashion industry, they would demand change as well.

As the brand has grown and become firmly established, they have also increased their commitment to sustainability as part of their mission as well. Protecting vital resources goes hand in hand with doing good for the people they employ. Recycling goods from paper to scrap metal and sourcing leather as a byproduct from the meat industry are just a couple of the ways ABLE seeks to be more environmentally responsible.

They continue to add layers to their mission over time, and it's beautiful to watch the evolution of this company. The big dream, Ward says, is to impact other global fashion brands by putting pressure on them to make changes in how they currently conduct business with their partners around the globe. By calling attention and raising awareness to those who could do better, Ward can leverage their brand's amazing support and growth potential to impact the world.

Starting with the simple act of training women to make scarves, the impact ABLE is making globally is tremendous. Building a fashion brand dedicated to these ideals might not have looked profitable on paper, but profits aren't always measured in dollars. The really cool thing is that ABLE proves you can actually do both.

> "What greater bliss than to look back on days spent in usefulness, in doing good to those around us."
>
> —DOROTHEA DIX,
> 19th century social activist and nurse

To learn more about our part in the community that's dedicated to doing good, scan the QR code.

SUSTAINABLE & ETHICAL PRODUCTION

WOMEN'S EMPOWERMENT

ABLE

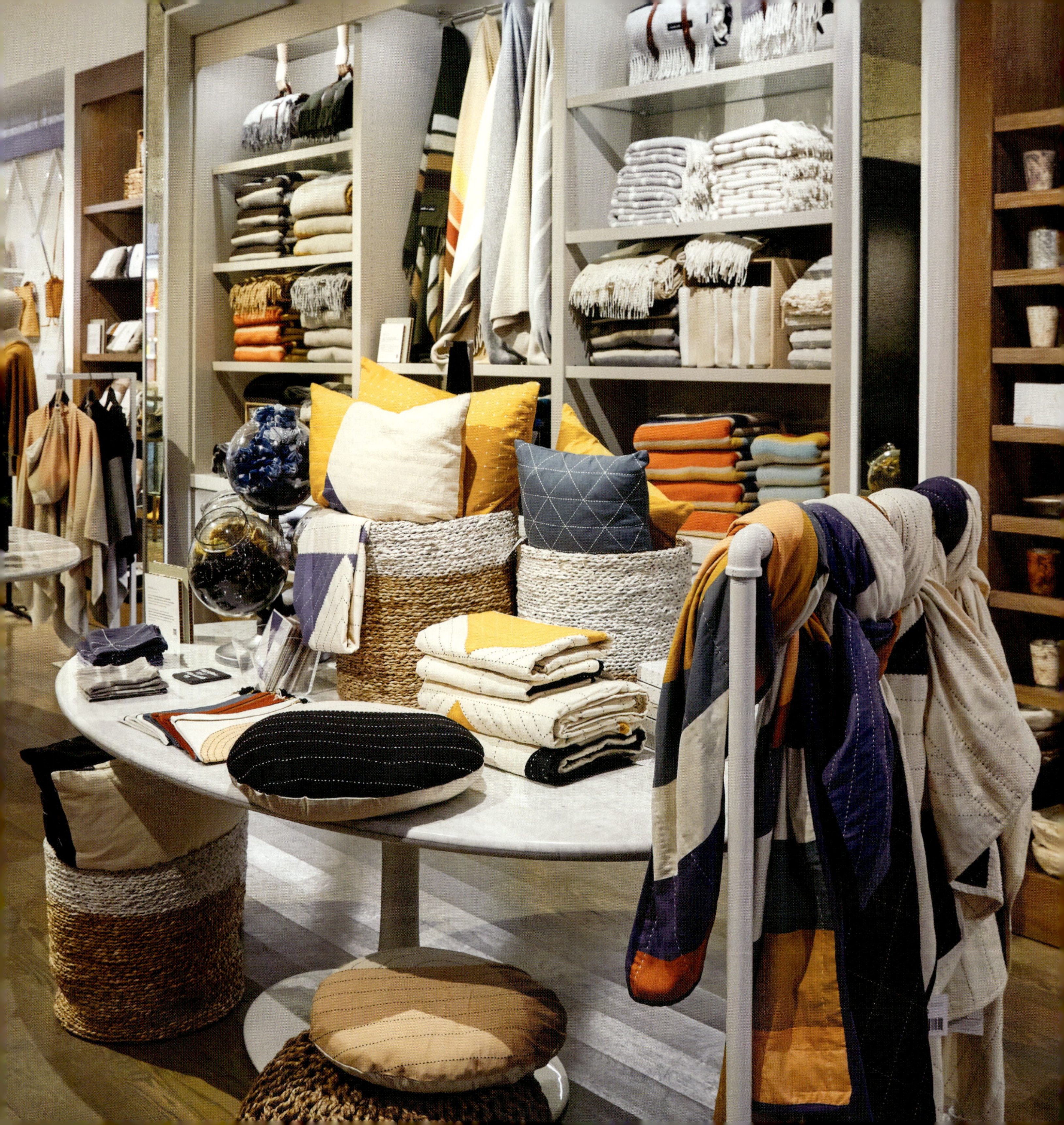

SUSTAINABLE & ETHICAL PRODUCTION

good

WOMEN'S EMPOWERMENT

Anchal

It all started in a design studio. Colleen Clines was taking a graduate seminar at the Rhode Island School of Design that took her on a trip to India in 2009. Through local leadership, Colleen was introduced to the exploitive world of the commercial sex trade and the lack of opportunity for women in the community. Inspired to design more than beautiful landscapes, Colleen determined to assist similar non-government organizations (NGO) again in the future.

While Colleen planned ways to collaborate with the amazing women she had met in India, her sister Maggie worked on environmentally conscious architectural projects in college. Maggie and Colleen traded stories on their design experiences and wondered how they could unite their passions to do good.

After returning home from that initial trip, Colleen and her classmates raised $400 by selling handmade notebooks and notecards. They used these initial funds to purchase a sewing machine, sewing instruction materials, and supply a stipend for the first collective of artisans.

In 2010, Anchal officially became a 501(c)3 non-profit partnering with a NGO already at work in India and by 2012, Maggie joined her sister to co-lead Anchal.

Anchal's first product was the quilt. At the beginning, making quilts was a simple way for the locals to begin earning money without years of expertise.

Quilts represent warmth and comfort. They are usable, functional, and flexible. Quilts born out of necessity and ingenuity from scraps of fabric are repurposed into something beautiful and new.

At Anchal, the designs blend the traditional, handmade craft with contemporary design—revolutionizing handmade textiles for the modern home. By challenging the textile industry's exploitative practices by investing in artisans and creating a human connection that extends worldwide, each design explores the relationship between art and storytelling. Bridging the gap between consumers and artisans leads to empowerment.

Kantha is the traditional embroidery stitch used for centuries by rural Indian women to

> "We felt compelled to take the project beyond the classroom with the conviction that our design training, in collaboration with local leadership, could address seemingly intractable social and environmental systems. The women we met became our sisters, sisters we had to fight for."
>
> —COLLEEN CLINES, *Co-Founder & CEO*

make quilts and other home goods. A simple craft to pass time or add a personal touch to one's home, kantha is a symbol of traditional Indian culture.

At its core, the kantha stitch is a simple running stitch that can be utilitarian in its most basic form—holding multiple layers of fabric together—or more decorative with overlapping, meandering, and filling shapes. The proverbial thread that ties it all together at Anchal lies in the use of this kantha stitching for each of their products.

Worn fabric and cotton saris are selected from vintage markets in India to up-cycle quilts. On average it takes an artisan *seven to eleven days* to make a quilt with around two hundred lines of traditional kantha stitching.

> "We both had linear projections for our careers. Then I saw that we could have more impact than I ever anticipated as a young woman. So I jumped onboard, and we decided to make a go of it!"
>
> —MAGGIE CLINES,
> *COO & Creative Director*

The leadership at Anchal devotes themselves to tackling social inequalities and reforming traditional textile manufacturing practices. A current problem in the "fast fashion" industry is that globally, humans consume about *eighty billion new pieces of clothing every year.*

A four hundred percent increase in the amount we consumed just twenty years ago.

From generating mounds of waste to fostering unethical labor practices, the fashion industry is also the second largest polluter. The harsh chemicals released during industrial dyeing damages aquatic systems and makes drinking water dangerous.

The marigolds have become an important symbol in this process. Anchal trains women to grow, harvest, and dye fabric with dye plants like marigolds grown through a network of urban gardens that were once vacant lots. This not only is better for the environment, but is a fulfilling process as well to work in the soil and produce these beautiful flowers which become such an important part of the textile projects in the future.

Anchal's mission is to address economic inequality faced by women around the world. With limited opportunity, this often leads to women being forced to make hard decisions in caring for their families. With no other means to earn a living, women find themselves forced into the commercial sex trade. With more access to educational workshops and a true living wage, Anchal provides a solution to this problem. This leads to transformation within the family and more broadly in the community at large.

To learn more about our part in the community that's dedicated to doing good, scan the QR code.

SUSTAINABLE & ETHICAL PRODUCTION

WOMEN'S EMPOWERMENT

Anchal

"Bel means 'beautiful.' Kai means 'ocean.' At the time, I was living just a few short blocks away from the beach. The ocean is just about my very favorite place to be, and I had a little one on the way, whose middle name is Kai. The name carries a lot of meaning for me, especially for that place & time of my life. And I think it has a nice ring to it!"

—WHITNEY WRIGHT

COMMUNITY DEVELOPMENT · good · FOUNDATIONAL FUNDING

Bel Kai

Founded in 2006, Whitney Wright launched Bel Kai with experience in hobby jewelry making. This hobby had progressed through many years and was a practical means of working through anxiety and depression at various stages in her life. Creating and crafting had always been a part of her childhood and young adult years. But paying bills and earning a living had always left it as a side hustle but much needed joy. Her need grew to launch her own business that would allow her the opportunity to stay home with her two young boys and the freedom to spend more time with them. Developing the skill needed to produce unique jewelry pendants, rings, and pieces of tiny art took time and practice, but Wright dedicated herself to the process learning and excelling along the way.

While creating and showing her collections at markets and craft fairs in the early years, Bel Kai grew and expanded exponentially. Creating custom jewelry allowed Wright the opportunity to produce special items that were one of a kind. This jewelry also met needs—not only for loyal customers but also for larger orders. These large orders came from non-profits and other businesses needing fundraisers. She finds great joy working on orders for these organizations and bringing attention to causes that matter.

By 2009, Bel Kai launched an online shop which expanded the reach of the custom jewelry business in a new way. In 2011, Whitney met her now-husband, Luke Wright, also an artist and the founder/CEO of MudLOVE. Their connection began through their businesses being incredibly inspired by each other, and it didn't take long to fall in love. Working together not only building business but also creating has been a catalyst for growth for each of them.

Their collaboration of brands has benefited both businesses as they have grown not only in their local Indiana community, but also as they reach across the nation both online and in brick-and-mortar stores. The spirit of doing good overflows and multiplies as the two continue to grow their brands and support other companies doing good as well.

BeLOVE is a local shop that they have launched as well where they can help friends and neighbors and give back to local needs in their own community in Indiana.

Their family has grown as well through the years with two more boys, making Whitney a busy boy mama who entrepreneurs and moms with the best of them. As anyone else who juggles this balancing act knows, it's busy and hard but something you wouldn't trade for the world.

> "The idea of community and helping others has always been a part of who I am. Growing up, my parents always made sure that my siblings and I were doing our part to serve our local community."
>
> —BLAKE MYCOSKIE, *founder of Toms Shoes, author, and philanthropist*

> "I don't think of myself as a powerful person. But I do use the platforms I have to make a difference in the world. Anyone who has a position where they can make a difference should use it."
>
> —SHARI ARISON, *best-selling author, businesswoman, and philanthropist*

Bel Kai continues to expand into new opportunities to build collections of jewelry, perfect for wholesale buyers. They love the opportunity to partner through products, especially when that means doing good with their partners or because the growth in business means more financial resources to bless others with.

COMMUNITY DEVELOPMENT

FOUNDATIONAL FUNDING

Bel Kai

To learn more about our part in the community that's dedicated to doing good, scan the QR code.

goodMRKT is a **connection**, an embrace of shared purpose. This is a **community** where makers and creators embody the challenges of the world and dare to make a difference. Where products with a purpose promote our common bond. goodMRKT is a **collective**, encouraged by a cause and dedicated to doing good. It is a **movement**, inviting you to discover something **new**, something **unique**, something... *good*.

"Our stories are what make us uniquely positioned to do something big in this world. We're the only ones who experience them. They're what give us passion and purpose."

—MICHELLE TUNNO BUELOW

FOUNDATIONAL FUNDING — HOMELESSNESS & HUNGER

Bella Tunno

"Buy one, give one" campaigns are not new in the purpose-driven business industry. It's a fascinating concept for most because it's a dual gift. When you make a purchase, whether for yourself or to give away, you are not only receiving a product, but you are also giving in a tangible way to a particular need or cause. Whether it's buying a pair of shoes or socks with an equal gift of shoes or socks in return or a purchase that supports a particular mission, the concept provides a rock-solid strategy executed so well by Bella Tunno today.

Michelle Buelow, the founder of Bella Tunno, has an interesting take on the "buy one, give one" model. While selling goods in this particular marketplace helps to immediately provide meals for children in need in this model, she's fueled by an even greater purpose to effect change on the larger issue of food insecurity for children and the impact and implication this has for adults who struggle with addiction. Her desire for this purpose-driven business is also one that hits close to home: the passion for this project began in 2005. She wanted to launch a fund to help vulnerable children. Being pregnant with her first child created the desire to help those much less fortunate than herself, and so she began this venture with the simple idea to sew bibs and burp cloths from her home.

Her products have evolved over the last sixteen years, but what has not changed is her passion for children outside of her home and circle. Her team has grown over the years, and they desire to make products that every mom wants in their own home. Buelow has infused her catalog with short and witty or inspirational sayings made to make us laugh or to start a conversation. Some of my personal favorite products are ones that state "world-changer," etc. Don't overlook the attention to detail in each of these products. After all, she's making products we will use in our own homes with our own children.

But there's more to this story. Buelow has always had ambition, desire, and drive for business, but in 2003, a pivotal moment occurred in her life. Her brother, who struggled with addiction for fourteen years, died. From this point on, Buelow was driven by the desire to leave a legacy for her brother—one that highlighted all the good things about him, not the addiction that took him from them. From this devastating experience, The Matt Tunno Make a Difference Fund was born.

Launching this fund launched the desire in Buelow

to do more, and she pieced together a way to make an impact in the two ways her passions were driving her. In her research she learned that one in six children went to bed hungry every night—that's thirteen million children! That's a devastating number to us who live in relative comfort and ease.

Yet there's a thread of connection here that you may not understand—food insecurity in children directly correlates to addiction in adults. Buelow's conclusion through all of her research was that in a fight to end hunger for children, she could, in effect, also reach a tangible solution to fight addiction in adults.

Because of this knowledge, Bella Tunno has had a singular mission since 2014. For every product sold—sippy cup, suction bowl, silicone bib, and more—Bella Tunno provides one meal. Every item equals one meal.

It's such an important part of the mission and vision of Bella Tunno that "Buy One, Feed One" is found all over their website and their product tags.

They have a meal counter at the top of the website which indicates close to nine million meals to date have been provided from the purchases that customers have made. Not only are the products amazing, but you also help the mission to end childhood hunger with your purchase.

It's a give-back business that's multi-faceted. It's a true collaboration between the customer and Bella Tunno, because as more individuals buy into the goal and make purchases, more can be done by this special community to end childhood hunger.

For every product sold—sippy cup, suction bowl, silicone bib, and more—Bella Tunno provides one meal. Every item = One meal.

Bella Tunno's mission is to make the world better, but let's face it, there are a myriad of ways that we can all take to try to accomplish this broad stroke. Pick an issue from hunger, homelessness, violence, addiction—all these tragedies need an advocate. But when trying to attack a problem head-on, one of the most challenging things to do is to stay narrowly focused. To this end, Bella Tunno is a certified B-corp. Because balancing profit and purpose is essential to this brand, achieving this certification assures consumers that oversight is being given to a corporation's social and environmental performance, its impact on workers and customers, and its continued public transparency. Utilizing the concept of business as a force for good, B Corps redefine success in today's marketplace.

Buelow has built not only a model that helps others, but she has built an incredibly successful business. Bella Tunno has not only award-winning products, but a founder who is a true leader in business.

She's a mom, a CEO, a driver for good, and she's been extremely successful with all of them. While the recent hard times in the marketplace have forced many out of business, she has doubled down her efforts to give back and supply food and jobs. Buelow's leadership and drive, shows that a business can do good and be successful in today's economy and should serve as inspiration to others to pursue the same.

To learn more about our part in the community that's dedicated to doing good, scan the QR code.

FOUNDATIONAL FUNDING

HOMELESSNESS AND HUNGER

Bella Tunno

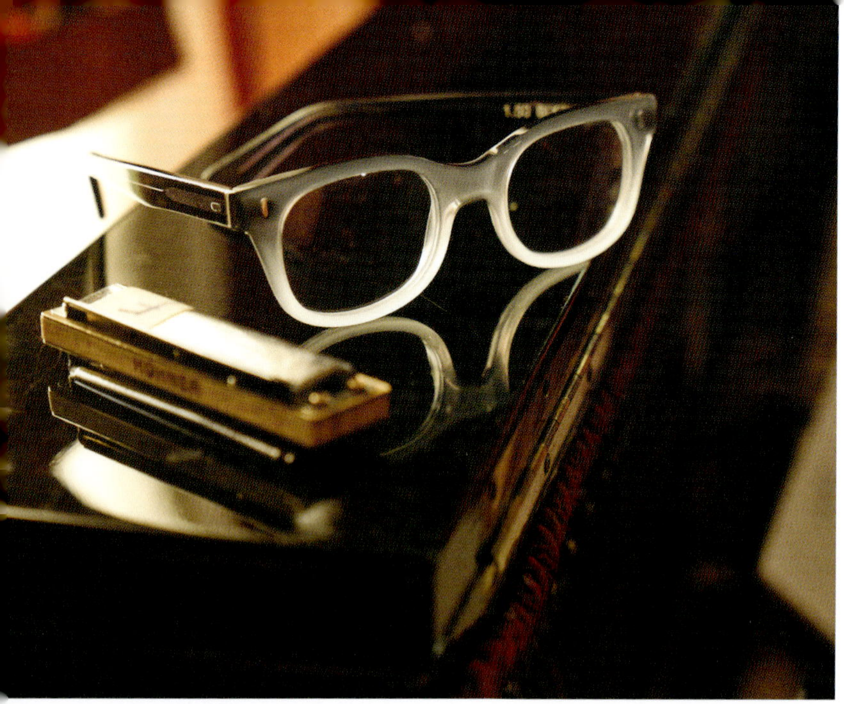

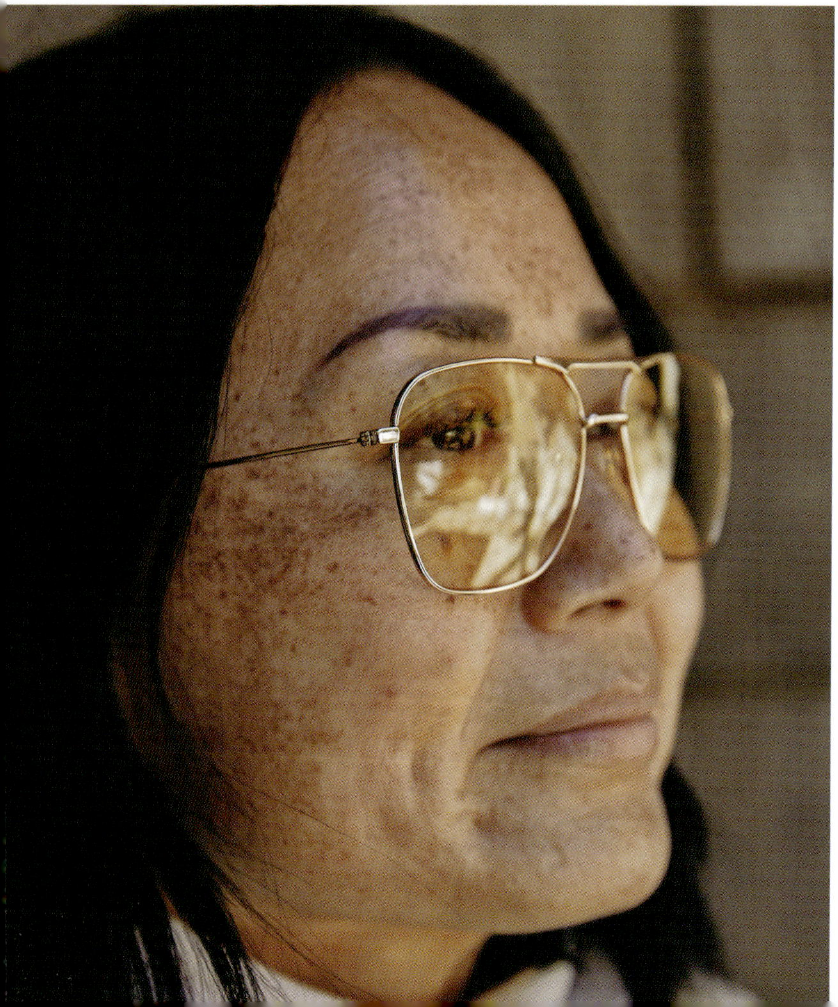

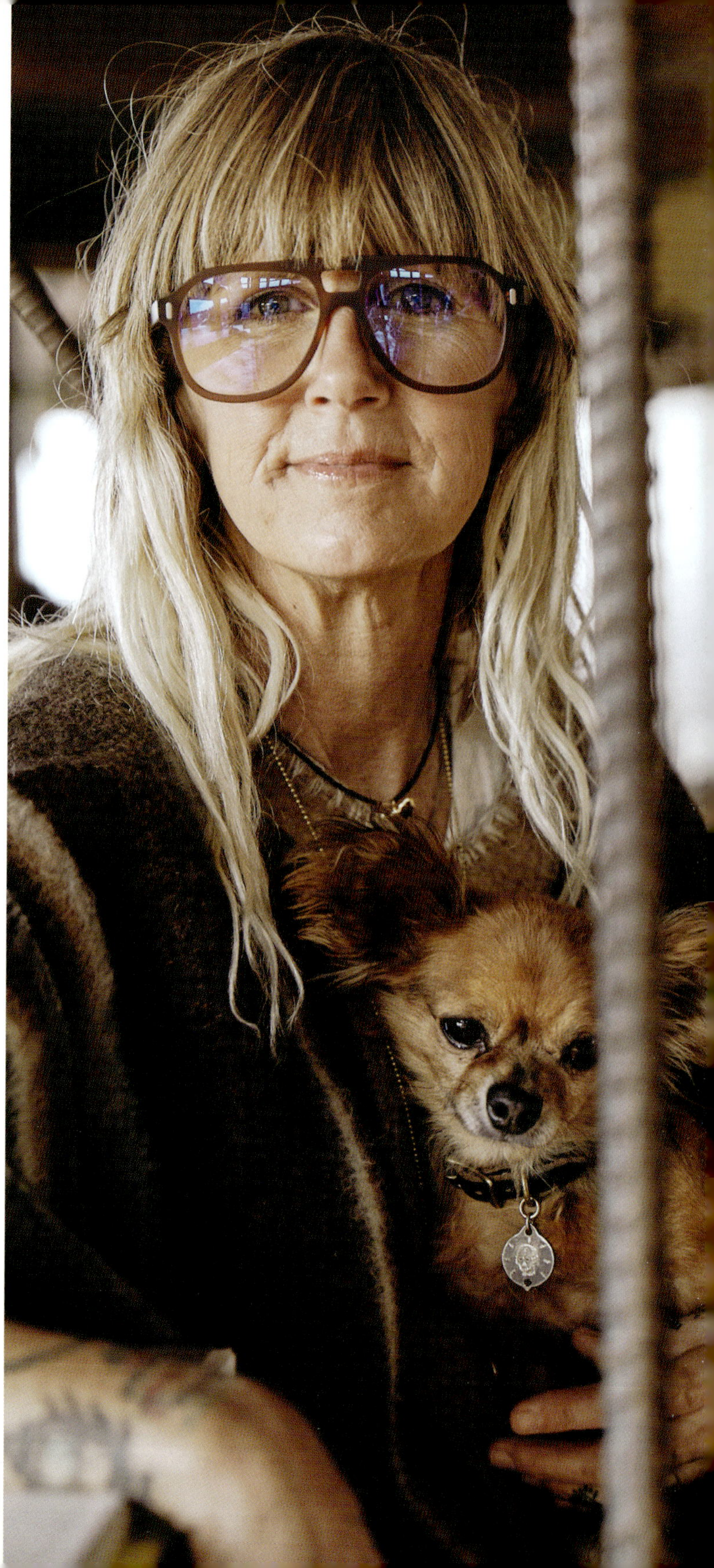

FOUNDATIONAL FUNDING

CADDIS

When a businessman decides to launch a new venture, he anticipates excitement over the products he is pitching. He would likely also expect a financial commitment to support getting that product to market. When that falls flat, though, and financiers don't catch the vision, he must either pack it up or start over again.

Early in the process of selling reading glasses to market, Tim Parr had a communication problem. After launching four startups previously, Tim decided when things weren't working to dig in and figure it out. He needed to understand why his potential investors didn't expect for anyone to spend $100 for readers, with a much better style, when they could just get some throw-away glasses at the grocery store for $10.

He learned that reading glasses and age go hand in hand. So building a lifestyle brand around glasses meant he'd need to have meaningful conversations about aging. And those conversations would need to be full of authenticity and transparency.

Unfortunately for him, the challenge was in recognizing the difference between the conversation that was occurring between investors and local creators. Parr decided to pursue building a lifestyle brand within his local skateboard, surfing, and music community, as they understood his mission more clearly. No one had approached aging in this way before.

And here's the reality—this product was and is needed. *Ninety percent of people over the age of forty will eventually need glasses in their lives because of an eye condition with no cure.*

Yet with all of this awareness and understanding of the problem, it took two years to raise the initial seed amount from individuals who understood the problem. The first check came after one investor had a dinner party where the conversation centered around reading glasses after trying to read the menu.

Why did Parr stay when it was not an easy path to success? A gut reaction of believing this was a need—that this product was better than other products on the market. Having launched other businesses, he recognized the same patterns that he had seen previously and knew he just had to persevere.

While readers and other eyeglasses are not new, the branding is what sets CADDIS apart. And this branding has made all the difference because of this mission to talk about aging. He enjoys using celebrity to bring everyone to the same level—we all have eye problems; we are all aging.

Another facet of this unique brand is its connection to music. As a former touring bluegrass musician, Parr's music roots grew deep. Originally thinking he could tour and run his company, he quickly recognized that that was not going to work after all.

Growing up in a musical family, he and everyone in his family played instruments. Even in elementary school, it wasn't "Will you play an instrument?" but rather, "Which instrument will you play?" Unfortunately those days are long gone, and the passing down of knowledge and collaboration that is often found among music communities is waning. Elementary schools lack funding to supply even the most basic

> "The purpose of human life is to serve, and to show compassion and the will to help others."
> —ALBERT SCHWEITZER, *Nobel Peace Prize winner, humanitarian and philosopher*

music lessons, let alone provide instruments for practicing.

So in addition to doing work to advance the conversation on aging, he also elects to give back to music programs. A stint at Patagonia working directly with Yvon Chouinard taught him all about the value of one percent. Being a business in the "for profit" sector that gave back could absolutely do good. One percent of gross revenue give-back programs can and do make massive impact and that is just what Tim aims to do. It was and is his why for being in business. The better the business does, the more instruments that may be purchased, and the more instructors can be paid. Working hand in hand with those who are already at work in these communities that desperately need the work and attention offers help to those who need it most.

Of course, success can also create more work. Success creates opportunity, so a needed expansion is underway to build a separate nonprofit. In this way, Tim can invite other brands to join him in making more funds and more opportunities available for children. These funds can go directly to counter the attrition of musicians due to lack of funding or the ease of gaming and lack of "cool" factor. The new entity is just being birthed, but the vision is to do more good by launching a separate arm that more people will want to be part of.

While CADDIS remains focused on the eyeglass business for now, helping people age gracefully through a system of readers to progressives and then bifocals—the recognition exists that more lies ahead. There is opportunity to tackle aging well with attention to other health and wellness categories that are different for an aging population compared to their twenty-year-old counterparts.

Parr recognizes that every growth conversation for this business means that success provides more opportunity to do good. And he's more than okay with that.

FOUNDATIONAL FUNDING

To learn more about our part in the community that's dedicated to doing good, scan the QR code.

CADDIS

C CRAVE Co.

C CRAVE Co.

C CRAVE Co.

CRAVE
Co.

Crave Candles produces **invigorating small batch soy candles, made locally in Alabama,** and steeped in the scents of the South.

good
SUSTAINABLE & ETHICAL PRODUCTION

Crave Candles Co

A booming business, today's candle market sales trend upward. With the candle market set to grow more than three billion dollars over the next few years, hobbyists might feel that they have nothing to offer. Lori Newell proves that's simply not true as her hand poured luxury soy candles are taking a bite out of the pie.

Newell took her hobby of candle making and combined it with her expertise in business to create Crave Candles Co, a growing brand presence in a crowded marketplace. Building products that bring people together is a large part of what drives her to continue to develop her brand. Born and raised in Birmingham, Alabama, Lori merged her passions into business as a single mom who desperately needed to make it work. She held onto the firm belief that she could not only sustain her family by building this business, but also impact others in her local community by creating jobs.

Today Newell's passion for creating products that bring people together centers around her knowledge of the value a well-scented candle can bring to a home. Building community, after all, should start in our own homes as we care for the people closest to us. The attention to detail from the choice of scent to the quality of the wax and containers used shines in her various lines.

A large part of Newell's candle making involves recycling. Her commitment to re-using and repurposing used bottles from wine and spirits keeps a focus on doing good not only in the jobs created but also in keeping more trash from the landfill.

When an entrepreneur begins the dream of launching a business from their kitchen, they can't always know quite how it will all turn out, but each one believes that they are on to something. Being able to execute her vision and dedicate herself to creating the best product she can has built Crave a faithful following and shelf space in over fifteen hundred retail outlets across the nation and provides private label candles for SAKS, Barnes & Noble, Cracker Barrel, and St. Jude Hospital. This growth wouldn't have happened, though, if she hadn't been willing to do the hard work—testing, experimenting, and failing. She worked local markets and festivals. When she wasn't selling, Newell took candles to her local stores and asked what they thought. Each time she received this feedback and worked it back into her products to continue producing the best available. This tenacity drove opening sales, and her quality products led to re-orders.

Her operation expanded from her kitchen over the years, and she's pleased to continue to impact her

> "Dare to dream,
> but please also do.
> For dreamers are many,
> doers are few."
>
> —BRAD MONTAGUE, *author and illustrator*

community for good through the continuation of job creation right there in Birmingham. Her entire manufacturing and shipping process takes place in her hometown.

Crave continues to grow through online sales, memberships, and corporate fundraising opportunities. Newell proves a successful business grows from passion and thrives as purpose to do good exists.

SUSTAINABLE & ETHICAL PRODUCTION

Crave Candles Co

To learn more about our part in the community that's dedicated to doing good, scan the QR code.

> You can become blind by seeing each day as a similar one. Each day is a different one, each day brings a miracle of its own. It's just a matter of paying attention to this miracle.
>
> PAULO COELHO

dōSA
Natural Skin Care Products

dOSA's handcrafted skincare products are toxic-free with plant-based colorants and are designed to deliver sustainable, skin-happy skincare.

With a focus towards generational stability, dOSA uses **profits from their organic skincare line to fund their not-for-profit, Future Cycle Breakers**, which empowers the disadvantaged youth who will be the future leaders of tomorrow.

SCAN QR CODE FOR BRAND VIDEO

SUSTAINABLE & ETHICAL PRODUCTION — good — WOMEN'S EMPOWERMENT

dŌSA Naturals

Low-income housing and the tough streets of Chicago were fertile ground for a force of future female entrepreneurs. An early start with teenage parents fighting addictions and challenges of their own added determination to these fiery ladies. Inspired by their second great-grandma Dosa McGee, dŌSA skin and body care products exists today in homage to what the influence one person can offer despite a tough upbringing.

Three sisters came together to launch a body care line with the belief that simple was best. Their great-grandma believed that everybody deserved happy skin! This idea became their mantra as the sisters created products only made with high-quality, environmentally-friendly, and socially conscious ingredients.

With determination to rise above humble roots, Charita, the eldest of the three girls, worked hard to overcome her starting obstacles. After spending thirty years in a corporate environment and finding herself in the boardroom at the highest point of her career, she recognized she wanted more.

First, she never quite felt at home among the rest of her peers. Recalling a time when publicly asked which person was their role model, many on the panel named people they had never actually met. Charita found herself thinking that her great-grandma was her role model and decided to answer truthfully, although she wondered about the value of her admission in that environment.

Second, she longed to do more with her expertise and experience in marketing and her desire to mentor the next generation. Something she couldn't see herself doing without making a drastic change to her life.

The avenue to do both things came through their new business dŌSA. While giving attention to the quality of the line of skin and body products with only nine or ten ingredients that were also undiluted and unpolluted, the sisters were intentional about leaving out one particular ingredient—*water*.

You may think that a bit odd, and in most skin and body care products it is unusual, but this became a key differentiator for dŌSA in a crowded market. Often brands that have eighty or even ninety percent water in them add chemical preservatives to prevent bacterial growth. Because the sisters wanted to have all natural ingredients, they simply couldn't add those ingredients and stay true to their mission.

In addition to the problems of a chemical additives, many countries face a global water crisis. Removing this element means preserving and conserving water for others who need the resource desperately.

Doing good for our skin and our earth isn't all dŌSA cares about either. Another essential element to the business of dŌSA—the opportunity to give back. Because struggle filled Charita's rise to the top she and her sisters desire to inspire and impact today's youth. Charita recognizes the value of having business and entrepreneurial role models since that was something she lacked growing up. No easy task, the sisters recognized that to break cycles of generational

> "Life's most persistent and urgent question is what are you doing for others?"
>
> —MARTIN LUTHER KING JR.,
> *minister and activist*

39

poverty they must plant the seeds of entrepreneurship in young people.

This intention led them to launch a non-profit initiative called Future Cycle Breakers with a sixteen-week workshop for children. Focusing on reshaping existing thought patterns, they work through all avenues of business education, including mindset. Educating children in everything from business practices to breaking cycles of self-doubt and learning to allow themselves to dream big dreams is a vital component of this program. Building communication skills requires practice in their learning program. The children practice these skills regularly by pitching their business ideas to entrepreneurs and venture capitalists. Teaching these business basics while children are young helps them pursue their dreams with confidence.

Proceeds from every sale that dŌSA makes are given to this program to raise up the next army of entrepreneurs ready to make the world a better place.

SUSTAINABLE & ETHICAL PRODUCTION

WOMEN'S EMPOWERMENT

dŌSA Naturals

To learn more about our part in the community that's dedicated to doing good, scan the QR code.

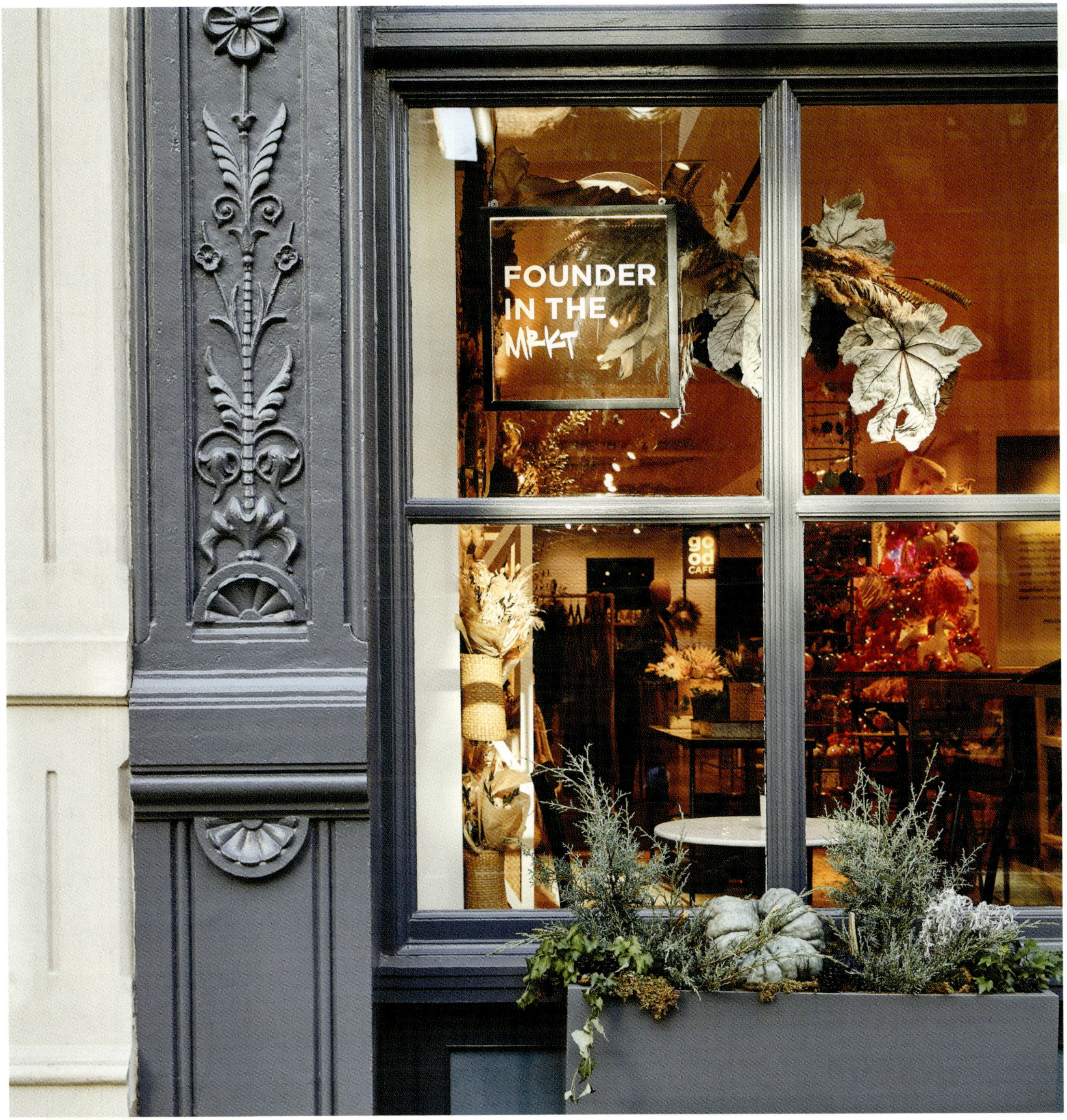
FOUNDER
IN THE
MRKT

FARMHOUSE FRESH

FarmHouse Fresh products are infused with house-grown vitamin and nutrient-rich extracts to awaken your youthful, radiant glow. Every product is grown using sustainable practices and each purchase helps to fund, rescue, and rehabilitate abused animals that their employees help care for at their sanctuary on the farm. FarmHouse Fresh is dedicated to their core principles: Grow Fresh daily, Spa Deliciously, and Rescue Fiercely.

ANIMAL RESCUE & SANCTUARY

good

SUSTAINABLE & ETHICAL PRODUCTION

FarmHouse Fresh

What did luxury skincare products and rescued farm animals have in common? Not a whole lot at first glance, but Shannon McLinden found a connection that gave her purpose. Finding a way to infuse that purpose into every one of McLinden's products at FarmHouse Fresh has been years in the making.

Having an entrepreneurial spirit at a young age often meant not fitting in with other children. Add to that a sense of individualism that marks most creators, and McLinden struggled early on to understand her place. Rather than excelling in school, McLinden found herself planning her next crafting project that she could then in turn sell to a friendly neighbor or friend.

Moving into writing and speaking, the then college-aged McLinden enjoyed any and every opportunity to create and share what she had made to help others and make an impact. Taking a job in advertising fresh out of school showed her that watching other people create while she tried to sell was not for her—she needed to be hands-on.

McLinden's aha moment came from trying to tinker around solving her own personal frustrations. As a runner who struggled to keep her heels from drying and cracking, she experimented with oils and sea salt until she found just the right combo. It kept her feet from cracking, and her friends loved it! Of course, the next logical move for McLinden built on the entrepreneurial spirit from her childhood combined with the advertising skills she had developed in that first job. So she launched a business around this foot scrub. This meant finding a manufacturer, creating packaging, and working on a hundred other details, but in six months, she became profitable—no small feat for a new company!

Since online sales were so strong and so many customers loved her product, she decided on a whim to package some samples. McLinden sent them out to different editors that were part of Oprah's team. McLinden knew that if she could get on Oprah's radar, business would boom. And sure enough, while McLinden continued to do the work over the next months, growing her small business, Oprah's team called to let her know that her foot scrub had made it onto Oprah's O List.

For McLinden, though, the newfound financial success was minimal in comparison to the validation and a sense of purpose that she now felt. The next piece of the purpose puzzle revealed itself soon after.

> "Doing good holds the power to transform us on the inside, and then ripple out in ever-expanding circles that positively impact the world at large."
>
> —SHARI ARISON, *best-selling author, businesswoman, and philanthropist*

As her business grew, McLinden became aware of how much she needed new hires. McLinden's first new employee was a fellow animal lover, and with a shared bond, they often helped rescue various small animals together as they encountered those who needed help along the way. As new employees joined the team, they found that there was a continued desire within each of them to not only help animals who were hurting, but also find a way to help the shelters who were providing care.

In a defining moment, Shannon recognized that they had certain capital reserves that could help shelters to build barns, or even better yet, provide resources to fund getting the animals from shelter to new home. In putting this money toward adoption events the following year, Shannon found the power in putting dollars where her heart already was.

While they continue today to work with rescues, she has big dreams of expanding future farm programs and providing kids opportunities to not only be around the animals, but to also learn about veterinary medicine and hopefully develop future doctors. Today the company's headquarters is home to its non-profit farm animal sanctuary that houses nearly forty horses, goats, donkeys and sheep. A portion of profits from skincare products goes toward all the animal care, and customers can track the batch code on their jar at the company's website to see the animal rescue activities they helped fund.

There have been many challenges in the business along the way, and McLinden readily admits that every step has been hard but rewarding. The recent changes brought on by the shutdown of hotel and spa industry for a time, have caused FarmHouse Fresh to move from an almost ninety percent wholesale model to an increased direct to consumer branding. Now at almost an even split between direct to consumer and direct to trade, McLinden proves again that she's not afraid to pivot her business strategies when necessary.

Her business continues to thrive and expand. As grateful as she is to be a successful businesswoman and entrepreneur, she appreciates even more that the increased finances mean the opportunity to give and do more good for the rescues that work hard but need funding to continue.

> "Giving feels good, but it's also good for the bottom line. Charity is a viable growth strategy for a lot of companies. Our customers get excited to be a part of what we're doing. If you ask anyone wearing Toms how they first heard about us, most won't mention an advertisement; they'll say a friend told them our story."
>
> —BLAKE MYCOSKIE, *founder of Toms Shoes, author, and philanthropist*

SUSTAINABLE & ETHICAL PRODUCTION

ANIMAL RESCUE & SANCTUARY

FarmHouse Fresh

To learn more about our part in the community that's dedicated to doing good, scan the QR code.

47

GENEROUS COFFEE CO.

DECAF

Medium Roast

Dark Chocolate | Brown Spice
Caramelized Sugar

Varietal Castillo, Caturra, Colombia

COMMUNITY DEVELOPMENT · good · SUPPORTING LOCAL ECONOMIES

Generous Coffee

A high school trip to a foreign country can change everything. In this case, it absolutely did change everything for Ben Higgins, because he left wanting to do something about the needs he saw. The seed planted on this very trip built in him a purpose he would later grow into. The need to build sustainable long term relief in needy areas versus focusing on disaster relief which is limited in scope, led him to conducting business in a new way.

As most business owners know, it's one thing to say you will do something, but it's a different thing to outline your intentions in an operating agreement. Generous was launched as a business that has in its DNA a plan to do good. This plan involves giving back one hundred percent of their profits to charity.

This means doing a whole lot of good.

Funding things like operating budgets, employee salaries, and the like may not be as exciting as other projects, but Higgins and his partners recognized there was a real need to focus their giving attention to just that. Often, it's not easy to ask people to contribute to salaries that pay reasonable living wages. Instead, it's easier to fundraise to dig a well instead of a distribution center.

So as Generous got its start, coffee was the natural go-to product for their catalog. Part of their brand identity was to sell something that brings people together and nothing does that better than a good cuppa joe. They operate on a lean business model, where they maximize profit potential and give back. This can help them to scale, but it's by no means an easy task.

Having worked with a roaster to supply their product in the past, they are now taking on the logistical responsibility for roasting, fulfilling, and supplying themselves so that they can continue to scale and expand. They are looking into corporate gifting, creating solid price discounts for schools and churches, and developing a very transparent lifecycle to see where the money goes and how it's impacting others.

As Generous Coffee has continued to grow and expand through the last few years, they recognize that coffee is not the starting and stopping point for what they want to do to help others. Rather they are just getting started.

While they intentionally travel to these foreign countries to find out exactly what needs exist and how to help, the last few years have created barriers to that. Higgins can't wait for that to change. Being on the ground in those countries is essential to building relationships with those local entrepreneurs.

Generous also wants to continue to develop their loyal fan base into true ambassadors. By building relationships, they will continue creating a lifestyle of generosity.

You may recognize Ben Higgins's name, especially if you are a twenty-something young woman. He achieved national attention after being on reality TV. This national spotlight caused his audience and platform to skyrocket along with Generous's influence and retail sales! But being on TV just for the sake of being on TV isn't Higgin's priority.

> "Yale University has estimated that innovators only collect 2 percent of the value they generate; that is, for every dollar an innovative company makes in profit, society has benefitted by fifty dollars. By becoming an innovative entrepreneur, you are, on average, producing benefits to society that far exceed your paycheck."
>
> —WILLIAM MACASKILL,
> *author and philosopher*

He sees no good in being a household name unless you do something to give back to this world.

As a purpose-driven business, Generous hopes to also encourage other larger corporations to get involved as well. As they continue to increase their volume of sales and create greater exposure in the marketplace, they'll have more ability to give to the projects they hope to fund.

This path to success hasn't always been easy. There were times when Higgins wondered if they could continue doing business in this way and sometimes bills would be paid just in the nick of time. With continued growth, Ben had to recognize when the time was right to bring in a CEO to run the day-to-day operations so he was free to continue using his time telling their story and leveraging his platform—this will naturally transfer to increased sales.

If you've read the other stories in the book, you'll know that Higgins also has connection to two other brands in this book—MudLOVE and Bel Kai. He knows Luke and Whitney Wright from their community in Indiana, and he even wore a Hope bracelet from MudLOVE on his reality show to remind him of home. It's good to see that purpose-driven businesses support and promote each other to do more good.

Indeed, this is something we can all aspire to by supporting each other in initiatives just like these.

Why does Higgins continue to do the hard work of selling and fundraising by having a purpose-driven business? "Because it's fun, and it's fun because it's hard." Hard work made more meaningful because it's good and does good.

To learn more about our part in the community that's dedicated to doing good, scan the QR code.

COMMUNITY DEVELOPMENT

SUPPORTING LOCAL ECONOMIES

Generous Coffee

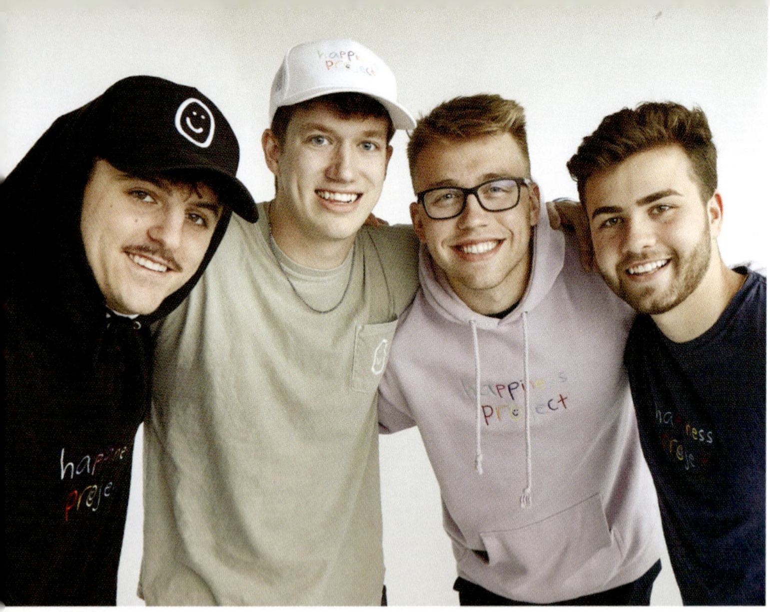

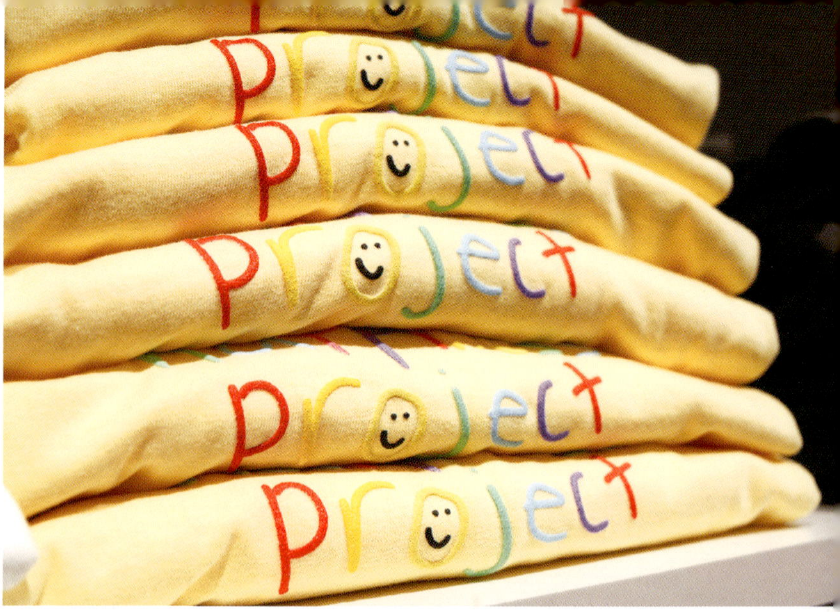
project

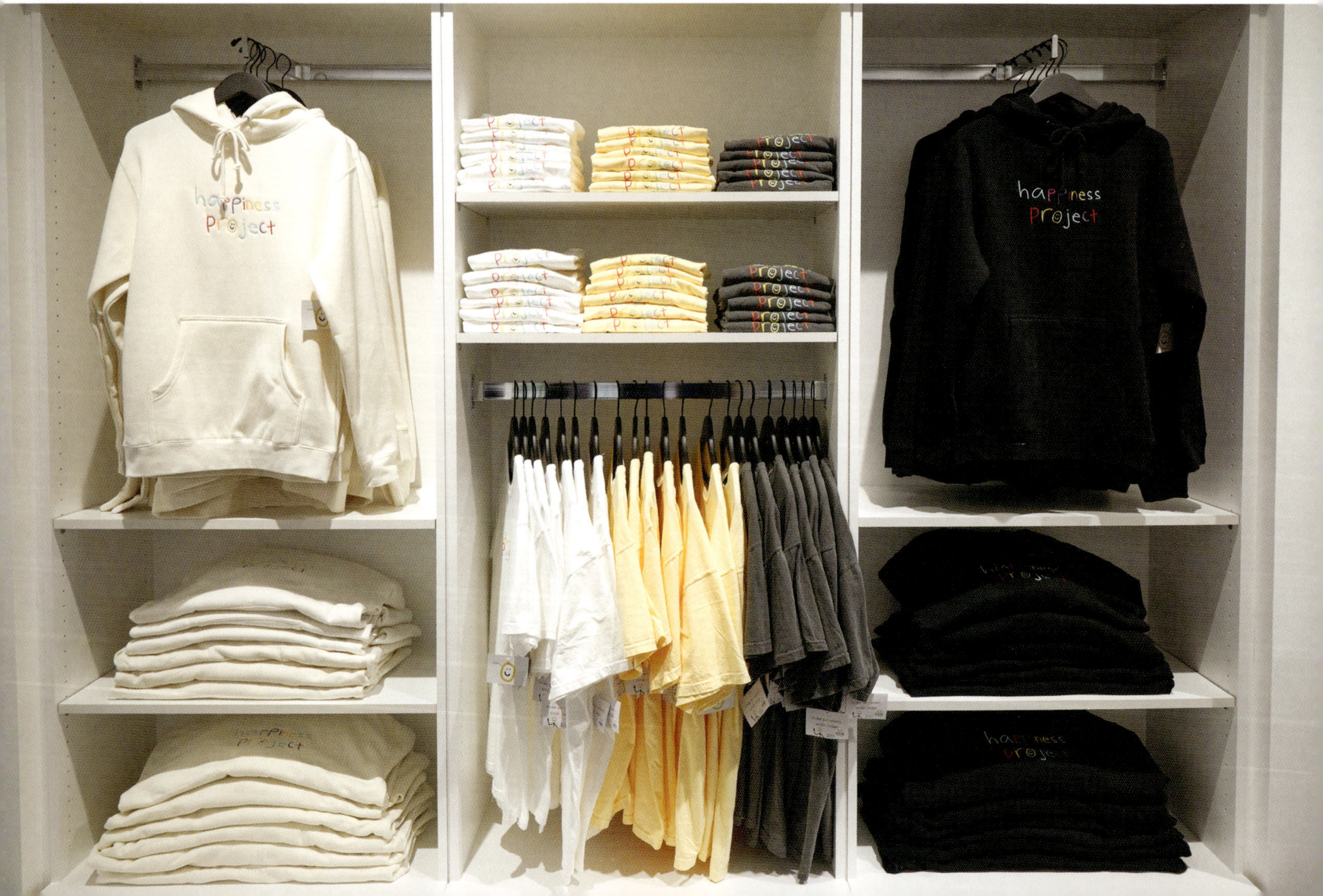
happiness
project

FOUNDATIONAL FUNDING

Happiness Project

Mental health is difficult to talk about. Luckily, that's changing as people become more comfortable discussing mental illnesses that are a very real part so many of our environments. Jake Lavin, founder of the Happiness Project, wants to use his brand to increase conversations around mental health. The more comfortable we are communicating these issues, the more comfortable people will be in seeking help.

That's the mission of Happiness Project—a clothing line that aims to "elevate happiness throughout the world" by increasing conversation and donating fifteen percent of their profits toward the American Foundation for Suicide Prevention.

Happiness Project has been around since 2017, but really started picking up steam during the summer of 2020. In 2017, one of Lavin's classmates, Nick Spaid, tragically lost his battle with mental illness. This event launched the mission of Happiness Project, encouraging Lavin to spread awareness about mental illness through his clothing line. By wearing a hoodie with "Happiness Project" emboldened

> "Doing good business—being ethical, being transparent, being caring, implementing values in your business—makes a difference, and you make money at the same time."
>
> —SHARI ARISON, *best-selling author, businesswoman, and philanthropist*

across it, it will prompt people to ask, "What is that?" Clothing provides a unique opportunity to talk about this unique brand and mental health in general. It's a great way to show compassion to others in a very genuine way by being willing to start the conversation.

The hoodies and other products are certainly cool, but the focus is always on the message and the mission. In 2020, Happiness Project donated over fifty thousand dollars to NAMI.org, the nation's largest grassroots mental health organization. NAMI is, in their words, "dedicated to building better lives for the millions of Americans affected by mental illness." Happiness Project gear itself opens conversations, but the brand does much more. The brand also donates fifteen percent of the proceeds toward organizations helping those fighting their battle against mental illness.

Happiness Project tested a plethora of hues before settling on the current pastel array you can see available on their website right now. They wanted to opt for "colors that scream happiness at you." Lavin hoped to keep the logo juvenile in a way, "almost like a kid writing it." It's an immensely serious topic, but by presenting it in a more relaxed way, it allows people to approach mental health with less hesitancy.

The long-term goal is to host festivals to raise awareness, get mental health resources into communities that can't afford them, and create a big factory-like space where people can have fun and hang out.

Between their donations and ability to spread their message, Happiness Project has made an incredible impact so far. The guys are passionate about not only growing their brand but their positive influence as well, so expect more from them in the future.

> "That's the mission of Happiness Project—a clothing line that aims to 'elevate happiness around the world.'"

By buying from Happiness Project, you are supporting young entrepreneurs while also aiding in mental health awareness.

The mission is to elevate happiness throughout the world, while supporting those impacted by mental health issues. No one must go through their journey alone. Happiness Project strives to show the world that it's okay to not be okay.

To learn more about our part in the community that's dedicated to doing good, scan the QR code.

FOUNDATIONAL FUNDING

Happiness Project

59

KaAn'S is an acronym—
Kenny Ashley Aiden and Noah—
the first letters of
each of their names.

WOMEN'S EMPOWERMENT

KaAn'S Designs

You can't ask for a better promo opportunity than to land on Oprah's Favorite Things List. Oprah recognizes talent, and this brand was chosen as part of her 2020 list. A business that gives back as part of its DNA, and you have a win-win in the baby and family apparel T-shirt business.

A wife and mama, Ashley launched this brand of tees with her hubby Kenny and three children. As a high school teacher, Ashley was looking at the time for an opportunity to come home to her growing family back in 2014. She had no idea that her search for a "mommy and me" T-shirt would land her a business idea. Or that that idea would connect with others looking for the same types of products. Recognizing the opportunity for a home-based business, and a potential side hustle in the making, the former teacher-turned-entrepreneur launched a lifestyle T-shirt brand. Keeping it simple with a small investment and a loan from her dad, the T-shirt business was born in their garage with their first sale arriving the same day they posted it on Instagram. By 2019, business had grown enough that Ashley was able to come home and work full time on the former side hustle.

KaAn'S (pronounced Can's) Designs targets the burgeoning market of millennial parents and their growing crew!

T-shirts, totes, and more speak parenting truths, which are sure to get a smile, especially from someone that understand the struggles. Pithy quotes aside, the products are made well and use high quality, comfortable materials, classic colors, and slick fonts. They have a loyal customer and fan base who also share the Greens's tight-knit family values and exuberant sense of humor. The attention and intention to represent diverse families make this brand appealing to a variety of people.

The creative styles are simple and hand lettered, but the combo is perfect for families.

Their signature set of T-shirts was designed for those with a lively, growing family. Featuring "The Original" (for the parents), "The Remix" (for the oldest child), "The Encore" (for a younger sibling) and "Mic Drop" (for a baby), each shirt comes in a variety of sizes for adults and kids, so that the set can be customized to different-sized households.

And that's not all—there is a variety of other styles for moms, dads, and kids. As business started booming, they expanded their inventory. Their expanded

> "Hope has two beautiful daughters—anger and courage. Anger with the way things are and the courage to make a difference."
>
> —JOHN MAXWELL, *bestselling author, coach, and speaker*

catalog adds sweatshirts, hats, pajamas, onesies, tote bags, and coffee mugs, all emblazoned with clever lines like a "Nothing In this Bag Belongs To Me" tote for moms, which is of course, a bestseller.

The internet has allowed customers to find and fall in love with Ashley's work. Their fan base is active on social media, and this connection with people, along with hope and hard work, continues to motivate her.

For Ashley Green, the secret to success is simple: many of the greatest ideas are found in your every day, i.e. my experience in motherhood.

And while seeing the business continue to grow is gratifying, for the Greens it's the balance and freedom their venture has provided that's been the real win. Ashley recognizes how KaAn'S Designs has helped her to realize her ambition of seeing a family like hers represented in the retail and social media landscape, all while allowing her to spend more time with the crew she loves the most. Giving back to her community is a byproduct of a successful business, since the more products are sold, the more jobs are created. She continues to inspire the next generation of young entrepreneurs to attempt whatever it is they can think up next.

WOMEN'S EMPOWERMENT

KaAn'S Designs

To learn more about our part in the community that's dedicated to doing good, scan the QR code.

65

be the
change.

blessed.
hope.

Mud
LOVE
ARTIST
SERIES
TAGGED
MUGS
MUD
PUDDLES

COMMUNITY DEVELOPMENT | FOUNDATIONAL FUNDING

MudLOVE

Luke Wright had a dream—make an impact in the world by doing something meaningful with his business. Not knowing where this vision would take him, he launched his business inside his garage with an old stamp set and a box of clay. Teaching ceramics to local fifth graders, he saw an opportunity to impact them by not only showing them to create, but also how to sell. In selling their creations, he saw the opportunity to encourage them to do good with their earnings.

MudLOVE bracelets began as Luke rolled out clay into round coils before pressing them and stamping in the iconic MudLOVE serif font with the words faith, hope, and love. He produced just about one hundred of these bracelets and put them out in his shop to see how customers would respond. After selling out in just a few days' time, Luke's test product was a success.

In a short amount of time, the idea caught on and demand increased. Like any other business when this occurs, scale must also accompany the need for expansion and employees hired. The team at MudLOVE expanded to a community with a passion for clean water.

MudLOVE donates a week of clean water for the people in Africa per purchase. Think about that for a moment: if I purchase a ten dollar bracelet from the good folks at MudLOVE, or any other product, they donate a week's worth of clean water to the people in Africa through the cooperative known as Water for Good.

Ten dollars.

Not only do you get an amazing inspirational product, but you also have the satisfaction of knowing that someone who didn't have clean water now has access to clean water for a week.

One bracelet. *One week.*

If you are anything like me, you want to buy five or one hundred, right? I mean ten dollars is not expensive in our society today. We easily spend more than this on gifts each year for birthdays, Christmas, Hanukkah, and more.

The intentionality afforded through purchases like this can be the great multiplier. The leverage that we find when a group of people come together collectively to influence and make a difference—*priceless*.

Through the years, the product lineup in the small ceramic studio in Warsaw, Indiana has grown and expanded. A catalog started as single bracelets now broadly covers coffee mugs, coasters, and other pieces you will want.

Everything they have is quality: these are not cheap trinkets or leftovers. This is purposing to do well from the very best, not the very least. MudLOVE is dedicated to creating products by hand and to be inspiring.

If you wonder why they supported water for Africa, it's simple, really. Without water, there can be no mud. Without water, it's not possible to create their products, and without water, it's not possible to sustain life.

From the beginning, MudLOVE was created to do good. The team at MudLOVE uses the tools they have to break continued cycles of hardship, poverty, and hurt. Further, they also believe if each person can be inspired, they each have something they can use to change the world.

Collaborations with others in our communities can advance the cause as well. An influential force like a celebrity from a reality show can make an amazing impact. Ben Higgins wore a blue hope MudLOVE band in 2016, and interest in the company exploded. Partnering with Ben, they provided jobs in Honduras and then launched an online fundraising platform. Their ideas had ideas, which created more ideas. Customers, by mid-2016, had raised three hundred thousand dollars for their needs from adoptions to medical emergencies. In using MudLOVE to raise funds, it's a double gift: clean water is still provided, and these fundraising efforts also benefit.

In 2017, they raised enough money to donate a new

maintenance truck to their clean water partner in Africa. By April 2019, they donated their one-millionth week of clean water, which amounts to four hundred and fifty thousand dollars.

Luke Wright and the team at MudLOVE prove that their compassion drives their passion. Their singular focus produces major results. Results that continue to make a massive impact on the lives of others.

To learn more about our part in the community that's dedicated to doing good, scan the QR code.

COMMUNITY DEVELOPMENT

FOUNDATIONAL FUNDING

MudLOVE

musee

Musee has been a guiding hand to Madison County, Mississippi with a mission of restoring lives by providing dignified work for vulnerable people in their community. With a workforce primarily made up of women in recovery, people with disabilities, and people who have lived in chronic poverty, Musee uses ethically sourced, natural ingredients to make handcrafted, organic bath products that are safe for all skin types.

good
SUSTAINABLE & ETHICAL PRODUCTION

Musee

The thread continues that we find in this book—*The product on the shelf is only half the story*. It helps you see what motivates and drives these amazing entrepreneurs to fulfill their mission in the businesses they launch and their passion to serve others.

It might be easy to overlook this work as you progress through the stories in this book because so many of these stories are similar. I encourage you to not let that happen. Each founder, each mission, and each motivation has a variation, while they might point to a similar purpose.

Despite the similarities or specialties, I think it is important to point out that this is still unusual in the world of business. A business is normally launched with the idea to make a profit. Some entrepreneurs enjoy this initial beginning of the business, getting something started completely from scratch, but after a while, they are ready to move on. They set about to find someone to buy them out and they move on to the next innovation. Some entrepreneurs know what a business needs to get to the next level. They are the ones that come in and continue driving forward making tough decisions, or accelerating changes that others need in order to move forward. Sometimes

> "The goal isn't how much money you make, but how much you help people."
> —BLAKE MYCOSKIE, *founder of Toms Shoes, author, and philanthropist*

businesses are launched because someone has a good idea, or a great product and they realize it can be more than a hobby. However, it's really a rare form for a business to be launched to try to specifically build people's lives.

Yet this is what we find in Musee's story: an amazing product line that stands on its own two feet among many of the most well-known brands in existence today. The beauty sector is a highly competitive market, but it wasn't a passion for the products in the beauty sector that launched this mighty empire. Rather it was the desire to help others find work.

A former congressman's wife, Leisha Pickering met various people in her public life. In these connections she realized that certain people have a harder time than others securing employment. Rather than just giving people some cash to help them out of their immediate challenges, the adage of "teach a man to fish" came to mind. So Pickering concocted a plan to launch a business of handmade items in the heart of Mississippi. Her focus was employment for those the system generally leaves behind—women in recovery, people with disabilities, and those who live in chronic poverty. She has also made it a point to employ those with felony records. The challenges are steep for those who are getting out of the prison system and are looking to take the right path when so many businesses refuse to hire those with a record. But this is precisely why Leisha has hired them. She looks for the potential a person has, not at their past. And while this does present its own set of challenges, it's also part of the reward.

So an idea was hatched back in a home kitchen in 2010. Leisha and her friend Adam set out to discover a handmade product that would also become a sustainable business. In addition, the product needed to be something they could teach others to make. After pulling out the kitchen mixers and playing with recipes, Leisha began making bath balms.

Because of her baking background, Leisha knew if you could get the ingredients right you would find success. She also believed that if she offered people the opportunity to turn their lives around while also making great quality products, she would soon have a winner on her hands. Starting at the local farmers market, the small idea gained ground quickly. Farmers markets, women's shows, and more were places where Musee's offerings really took off. Boutique stores and a storefront were even added along the way. And as a reminder to not despise small beginnings, a trip to the Atlanta International Gift Market really sent the business rocketing forward. By 2018, the balms were available in more than thirty-five hundred stores and spas across North America. They sold more than three million bath balms through 2018. By 2019, Musee became the largest wholesaler of bath balms in the country!

Musee has greatly expanded through the years. They continue to upgrade facilities and increase opportunities by expanding not just the facilities but also the products. Pickering also sees the products as an opportunity to encourage others with packaging that offers words of hope and inspiration.

If that wasn't enough, all of Musee's products are ethically sourced with natural ingredients. It's a significant factor that the beauty care routine they provide is safe for all skin types, so it must also be sulfate and paraben-free.

It's safe to say—buy the products. The part that adds so much power to the mix—knowing that your purchase supplies jobs. Each purchase makes a tangible difference in the life of someone who but for the grace of God could be me.

It's such a beautiful thing because the purchase isn't only because it does good, it's also because the product is amazing. It's such a win-win!

It's exciting to note as well that Musee helps far from home. Musee has invested its profits into providing resources to international organizations that support schools in Haiti, orphanages in Africa, and Syrian women and children refugees. The funds help provide teacher salaries, books, desks, and meals as well.

The mission abroad and at home in Mississippi is pushed by the generosity of a CEO who saw a bigger picture than a product on a shelf. The tangible change in a person's life is a return not many get to take part in.

And honestly, that's a whole lot of return for a bath balm that makes me feel good too.

SUSTAINABLE & ETHICAL PRODUCTION

To learn more about our part in the community that's dedicated to doing good, scan the QR code.

Musee

"Nobody made a greater mistake than he who did nothing because he could do only a little."

—EDMUND BURKE, *statesman, economist, and philosopher*

SUSTAINABLE & ETHICAL PRODUCTION — good — WOMEN'S EMPOWERMENT

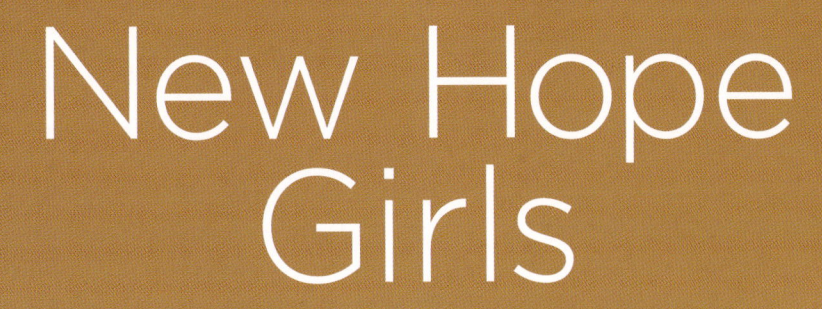

New Hope Girls

From its very inception, New Hope Girls exists because of the massive demand for help and hope. Because the needs are vast and overwhelming, it's easy to throw our hands in the air and give up. After all, we can't help everyone. But the truth remains that those who make an impact in this world by doing good recognize just because they can't help everyone doesn't mean they shouldn't try.

Only doing a little often feels worthless. It seems as if we are throwing one pebble into a sea, hardly making a splash, and then it's gone. But if each committed to reaching one person, we could easily solve many of the crises in this world. All it takes is one person.

Joy and Vidal Reyes and all the workers who assist New Hope Girls in the Dominican Republic make this their mantra. The Reyes' replanted their lives from Idaho to the Dominican Republic because of their desire to do just this.

What began as a shack on a hill in the barrio of La Vega has grown to two private homes today. These homes and their staff care for all the girls' needs.

Girls come to New Hope with many needs. The most immediate is usually physical rescue. A safe and secure home away from those who wish to harm them can be the first step in helping these girls begin to thrive. The nasty underbelly to the beautiful island nation remains sex tourism. To understand this issue more fully, you need to know that the Dominican Republic ranks number four in the world for sex tourism. The average age of girls and women who are trafficked is far lower in this area of the world than in other locations. Girls, ages eight to twelve, are routinely sold by their family many times because of poverty. They are trafficked not only to the sex trade on the island but also around the world.

Think about that for a moment. Girls *eight to twelve*.

The necessity for rescue remains great and if we aren't careful, it is easy to become overwhelmed by the statistics and the size of the problem. Rather, we should dig deep and figure out how we can help too.

After providing refuge for the girls, the Reyes' expanded their vision. They realized they could also help to facilitate change by figuring out how to help the women stuck in this cycle, many of whom were themselves trafficked. The pattern continues because the women, in desperation from either continued physical abuse and violence or poverty, will sell their own daughters. Without intervention, this cycle will continue from generation to generation.

An idea was formed and executed with the help of a volunteer who opened her home to the fledgling organization. Providing jobs to the women who found themselves hopeless played a key role to this intervention. The Reyes' set out to create something new from what was discarded and worn. Putting to work the women in the community who needed jobs, these hard workers began making purses of all shapes and sizes from old pairs of jeans. Sewing machines were then purchased as they could afford them, and soon the New Hope Girls purse business launched. This dual-purpose

> "There is physical evidence of the body's response to doing good. Endorphins are released in the brain when you do something for someone else. Doing good really feels good."
>
> —EVELYN LAUDER, *businesswoman, socialite and philanthropist*

engine not only provides jobs and income for those who need it most but also supplies a means to support the ongoing work of rescue there in the Dominican Republic.

Recently seeing their first graduate from the home, New Hope Girls continue with their expansion plans. As more and more girls are successfully rescued, provided refuge, and given resources to thrive, more girls will graduate and move into a brighter future. Many have already started giving back by working with the new girls coming in and by helping to break the cycles that have enslaved them.

It is amazing to look back and see how much has changed through the years for New Hope Girls. The expansion because of the mission and vision of the Reyes' is breathtaking. More girls helped, more women employed, more support and funds raised because of it.

The message of "Created for More" permeates every fiber of the work here. The daily labor to provide refuge and rescue for girls and women in danger is far bigger than many of us can understand.

Anyone who encounters the New Hope Girls mission and vision cannot leave unmarked. Many become continual supporters by either making regular donations, contributing to capital fundraising opportunities, or being a faithful shopper of bags that are still being handmade in the Dominican Republic today.

It's a beautiful thing to do what you can with what you have. For the Reyes', it required a move and being on the ground. Doing what you can with what you have requires thinking outside of the box for solutions that will impact not only the present but the future as well.

To learn more about our part in the community that's dedicated to doing good, scan the QR code.

SUSTAINABLE & ETHICAL PRODUCTION

WOMEN'S EMPOWERMENT

New Hope Girls

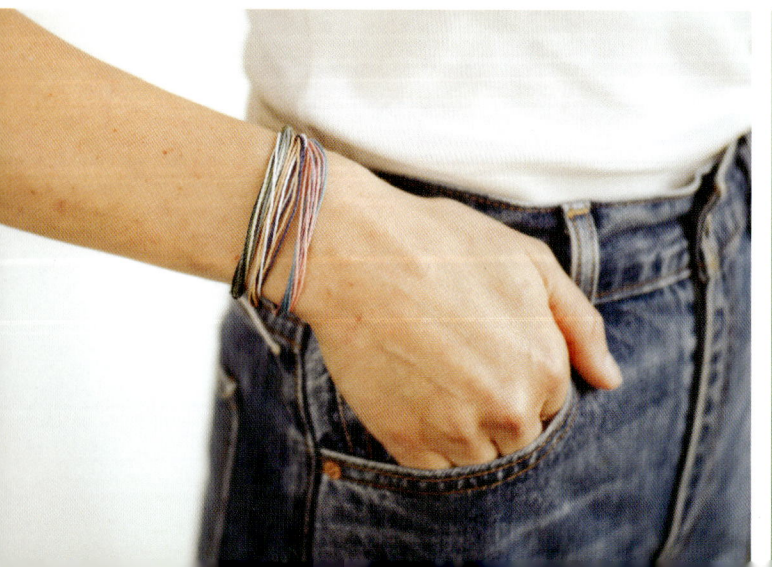

Pura Vida, or "pure life," is all about a lifestyle that Griffin Thall and Paul Goodman had found in Costa Rica themselves. An easy pace, enjoyment of life's deepest and greatest pleasures, and slowing down to enjoy life to the fullest.

FOUNDATIONAL FUNDING — good — SUPPORTING LOCAL ECONOMIES

Pura Vida

The mission for this organization is simple—to give back. But the implications and possibilities are vast. Implementing this corporate strategy comprises three arms—provide sustainable employment for artisans, give back to charities, and protect the planet.

Griffin Thall and Paul Goodman, the founders of Pura Vida, pursue these efforts to provide sustainable employment in artisan communities, by establishing partnerships that are global—from San Salvador, Dongguan, New Delhi, and beyond. Hundreds of people benefit from this employment.

Never imagining a summer trip to celebrate their college graduation in 2010 would result in a vision for a new business, Thall and Goodman thought their tropical location was just going to be a good time. Today's Pura Vida was born along the gorgeous beaches of Costa Rica among a people that were easy to love. In a single act of kindness to help the local artisans, these men commissioned an order of four hundred string bracelets with which they would return home.

What they didn't realize though was that this one simple act of doing good, was in reality a smart business move. Selling out within the first couple weeks of their return, they realized they were on to something much bigger than just a friendship bracelet. Pura Vida, or "pure life," is all about a lifestyle that they had found in Costa Rica themselves. An easy pace, enjoyment of life's deepest and greatest pleasures, and slowing down to enjoy life to the fullest.

What started as a few bracelets a week in sales has now become a worldwide movement, with *millions* of bracelets sold each year.

Without customer buying support, there would be no opportunity for expansion or employment of others in this endeavor. There are over eight hundred artisans in countries around the world that can count on a steady income and a positive work environment because people buy bracelets.

> "We should certainly feel outrage and horror at the conditions sweatshop laborers toil under. The correct response, however, is not to give up sweatshop-produced goods in favor of domestically produced goods. The correct response is to try to end the extreme poverty that makes sweatshops desirable places to work in the first place."
>
> —WILLIAM MACASKILL,
> *author and philosopher*

And once again, if the product wasn't any good, this would be a hard sell. But the products are great, and they appeal to a young demographic, who prove that they love this give-back model. The fact that their dollars can go further by buying things they want and also help others with those purchases resonates with our younger generation. If the products weren't appealing, there would be no way to bring attention to the different causes they support or help the artisans they have employed. Sourcing items from sustainable materials with socially conscious or fair-trade factories is one part of the process. Understanding how to continue to scale this growing business and being able to give back more because of the growth is the other.

And listen, the mission doesn't stop there. Giving back is a core principle for Pura Vida. They created a special collection that has helped over two hundred charities and donated almost four million dollars to causes we all know and care about. Breast cancer awareness was the first charity connection, and now, it's a major brand purpose to create special bracelets for collaborations that help give back to other mission-driven brands and businesses.

Retailers support their efforts by putting the bracelets in stores. Customers support the retailers and Pura Vida by buying more bracelets. Everyone wins because in the end, the artisans can have a sustainable income and provide for their families when they might otherwise be homeless.

To learn more about our part in the community that's dedicated to doing good, scan the QR code.

FOUNDATIONAL FUNDING

SUPPORTING LOCAL ECONOMIES

Pura Vida

For over 30 years, Raggidy Edges has been using vintage American and European materials to create gifts and accessories specifically designed to help non-verbal and language-delayed learners. Dissatisfied with the lack of accessibility in teaching methods for these learners, Cindy Roberts began creating products using recycled materials inspired by the tactile-learners she worked with as a speech pathologist.

EDUCATION & THE ARTS

Raggidy Edges

Just what happens to old decaying bedspreads, quilts, and other well-loved fabrics when they are no longer wanted? How do you preserve a sense of history and connection to the past without becoming a hoarder because you want to keep all the things? Keeping items—furniture, accessories, and yes, even certain blankets and cloths—can help us keep a connection with our heritage. By giving new life to these precious items through refurbishing or reinventing, we also preserve memories.

While we often see the DIY and renovation of large items, we don't often consider what happens to vintage fabrics when a large piece can no longer be used the way it was once imagined. Because of the changes in the way we gin cotton, blankets, and bedspreads no longer break down like our older, vintage pieces do. To prevent these items that have been well-loved through time from ending up in a recycling bin or trash can somewhere, Cindy Roberts breathes new life into special creations that preserve vintage fabrics and styles to provide tangible, tactile keepsakes at the same time.

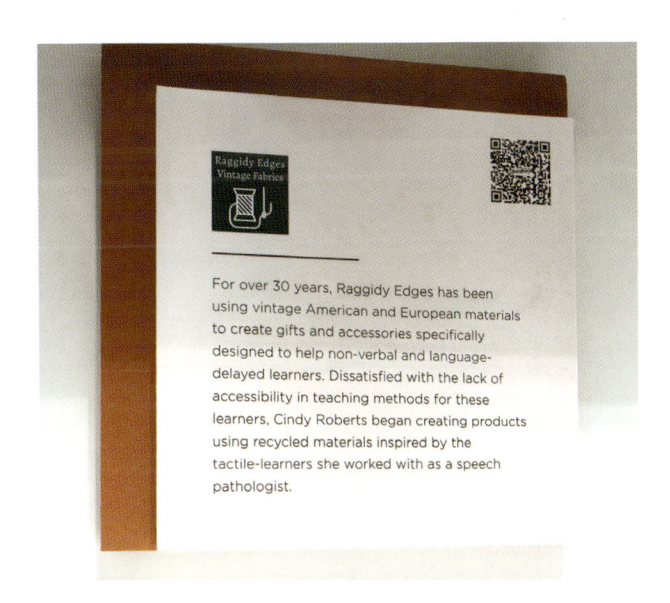

> For over 30 years, Raggidy Edges has been using vintage American and European materials to create gifts and accessories specifically designed to help non-verbal and language-delayed learners. Dissatisfied with the lack of accessibility in teaching methods for these learners, Cindy Roberts began creating products using recycled materials inspired by the tactile-learners she worked with as a speech pathologist.

"I think sometimes we forget what we have, and occasionally it's important to remind ourselves."

—BLAKE MYCOSKIE, *founder of Toms Shoes, author, and philanthropist*

The process began over thirty years ago as Roberts worked with non-verbal and language-delayed learners as a speech pathologist. Seeing a lack of opportunity and a big disconnect in teaching methods, she turned to tactile fabrics and craft projects to refurbish individual items into unique and special gift items to assist in the learning process. Because so many of the students learned best through touch and benefited greatly from tactile learning systems, she created projects tailored to fit the learning needs of each child. When other teachers began to ask about purchasing some of the projects that had been crafted, the idea for Raggidy Edges was born.

A divorced, single mom, Roberts made the leap to go all in on her passion to refurbish and recreate for sale. While it may not have made a lot of sense to make such a big career change, the timing was right to take a year to see if she could make a successful business out of her idea. Living with her parents at the time gave her the room to make the move to see where this idea could take her.

What happened has been so beautiful. Not only was she able to provide for her family, she created a certain amount of independence for herself as well. Being free to be home when they were home, or to go to school functions and games, or travel as an entrepreneur, allowed this mom to be involved in every way as she raised her family.

> "I believe that every human mind feels pleasure in doing good to another."
> —THOMAS JEFFERSON, *statesman, philosopher, and Founding Father*

While there have been some missteps along the way, Roberts chalks all of it up to a learning experience about what she wants for her business and doesn't. Because many of her designs require her to be hands-on, at least with the final construction, she recognizes this does limit her scalability. Even so, this is an intentional choice, as she doesn't want to lose the creativity of the process or the thrill of finding the fabrics and bits and pieces used to create the precious creations.

Even better, as she has grown this business through the years, she has been able to quietly and behind the scenes set up anonymous scholarships for those in her community and other areas to receive what they need for their education, from school supplies to tuition payments.

She exhibits regularly in market shows to the trade and in arts and crafts fairs sharing some of the creations with audiences and supporters around the world. She also enjoys teaching others not only how to create beautiful keepsakes but why it's important to do it as well.

EDUCATION & THE ARTS

To learn more about our part in the community that's dedicated to doing good, scan the QR code.

Raggidy Edges

OLD FASHIONED

barrel-aged bourbon / oak / demerara sugar / orange citrus

SCENTED CANDLE HAND POURED IN WHISKEY GLASS - SOY WAX BLEND - 8.5oz - 240g

RANGER STATION
NASHVILLE, TN

HEY RANGER!

LISTEN UP,

YOUR CANDLE IS POURED INTO A WHISKEY GLASS, SO DON'T GO THROWING IT AWAY ONCE IT BURNS OUT!

RATHER, GO TO O... "CARE" FOR INS... THE GLASS TO ... VESSEL!

YOUR CANDLE ... COCKTAIL REC...

LIGHT YOUR ... MAKE SOME...

DON'T WOR... THE RECIP...

HTTPS://RANGERSTA...

RANGER STATION

good

SUSTAINABLE & ETHICAL PRODUCTION

Ranger Station

Steve Soderholm launched Ranger Station, a high-end fragrance brand, from a hobby that began in his home kitchen. As a working musician, Steve found himself traveling around the world often, but missing his home in Nashville. The ever-increasing pull of setting down roots and being home along with an equally strong desire to truly cultivate a gathering place for friends and family forced him to consider a lifestyle change.

Of course, crafting candles and launching a brand was not what he had envisioned doing when he stopped doing gigs. Yet that's just what happened when a fun hobby became a means to having a meaningful career and an opportunity to employ others much like himself in need of a job from time to time.

Having spent his childhood in the North Woods of Minnesota, certain fragrances brought sweet memories back to him. As Soderholm started experimenting and making candles for his own enjoyment and joy, he tried to reproduce those fragrances. Little did he realize that he had a money-making venture right under his nose.

This idea for creating candles in reusable cocktail glasses started as a hobby but he soon mastered the fragrances he always dreamt of finding in the store but never could. Soderholm found that using cocktail glasses as his vessel of choice created both a reusable container and a collectible at the same time. It didn't take long to become more than a hobby. After making candles for friends and family, he realized the potential for selling them as a side hustle. And that's the simple start to growing a budding business.

Recognizing his ability to make a living with this once-side hustle, Soderholm also saw the opportunity to provide employment for other musicians who, like him, would be on again/off again based on their road trips and working gigs. This gave him a new opportunity to settle down and settle in to a new life off the road.

Ranger Station believes the currency of our lives lies in our memories and experiences.

> **"To be doing good deeds is man's most glorious task."**
> —SOPHOCLES, *ancient Greek playwright*

One of the greatest connectors for us into these memories is our sense of smell.

So the mission remains simple: make sustainable, handmade fragrances that are developed safely and cleanly, so they are not only good for you but also the environment.

Their mission to be sustainable and all-natural is not unique, but there is some discrepancy sometimes in what "all-natural" really means. Society often tells us that this designation is the healthiest and safest way to go, when many natural ingredients are toxic, endangered, animal by-products, or a combination of these. At Ranger Station, they

> "Exercise your purchasing power as a consumer, volunteer and bring joy to those in need, and share your experiences, tell your stories, and inspire others along the way."
>
> —BLAKE MYCOSKIE, *founder of Toms Shoes, author, and philanthropist*

have expanded their mission specifically by using ingredients that are both safe for you and for the environment. This means that they use all natural materials when they can, but if an ingredient is toxic or cannot be sustainably sourced, they use the synthetic alternative which is safe and sustainable.

Ranger Station is also growing its product line into fine fragrances and personal care items so that you can take your favorite scent with you wherever you go. It's exciting to see what might lie ahead for this brand. After all, the sky's the limit when you love what you do, you are committed to healthy and sustainable practices, and you do good for those who need it.

SUSTAINABLE & ETHICAL PRODUCTION

Ranger Station

To learn more about our part in the community that's dedicated to doing good, scan the QR code.

101

"May you always be the one who notices the little things that make the light pour through, and may they always remind you: There is more to life and there is more to you."

—MORGAN HARPER NICHOLS,
artist, poet, and musician

EVERYONE IS SOMEONE

FOUNDATIONAL FUNDING | good | HOMELESSNESS & HUNGER

Sackcloth & Ashes

A mom who was homeless. A son who cared.

It's a simple story, really, without an easy solution. Homelessness occurs in the United States today at a rate of seventeen people per ten thousand. The causes are many: PTSD, poverty, mental health issues, and more.

So when Bob Dalton decided to impact homelessness, it was personal. It's the effect of a mother's love and a son's connection. A son who cared enough to help not only his own mom, but other moms and sons too.

In 2014, Dalton decided to call local homeless shelters to get an idea of what their greatest need was. Inspired by his mom's journey, he thought he could help fill a need. What was unexpected was that they all responded the same way: they needed blankets.

Knowing what the need was, he began a mission that is ongoing and growing today. Sackcloth & Ashes was founded to help provide for this common necessity among the homeless population. The mission is clear—for every blanket purchased, one is donated to a homeless shelter. *But there's more*. The beauty of Dalton's mission is that he takes it one step further.

This blanket donation is not just random—it's not just donated to a local shelter near Sackcloth & Ashes. Instead, the blanket is provided to a shelter in your zip code, giving you the unique opportunity to bless someone nearby, a very real need in your own community.

Talk about impact.

Sackcloth & Ashes works in a variety of ways. One is to highlight grassroots organizations that are creating solutions for helping the homeless. Partnering with these teams demonstrates the tremendous power in collaboration. In addition, the blankets that are donated, although a real and practical need, are just one of the things that connect Sackcloth & Ashes to amazing people and organizations doing incredible work on a grassroots level.

 If you read between the lines, you'll see that Sackcloth & Ashes wants a little more from you than just a purchase. When they donate a blanket after your purchase, they hope you'll take it to the next level and begin to work in your own community, loving the people who are struggling right there where you live.

A forward-thinking business that not only gives as much away as it sells but also encourages community support, care, and concern, Sackcloth & Ashes models taking charity a step further.

They set ambitious goals too. In 2018, they set a goal to launch one million blankets to local homeless shelters by 2024.

It's a gift with a purpose and story. These blankets are a purchase that you will not regret. They are beautiful and feel amazing to the touch. The fabric is manufactured in Italy and the United States and have an added benefit of being from one hundred percent recycled material, eco-friendly, and good for the environment. Each blanket is ethically made and produced in Oregon.

In partnering with Native Americans for many of the designs for the Heritage Collection, Sackcloth & Ashes continues its mission of sustaining local artisans and economy.

Doing good means growing from our pain and reaching out to give it purpose.

> "The more we focus on issues, the more issues we create. The more we focus on solutions, the better society we create."
>
> —BOB DALTON

To learn more about our part in the community that's dedicated to doing good, scan the QR code.

FOUNDATIONAL FUNDING

HOMELESSNESS & HUNGER

Sackcloth & Ashes

spoonful

Artist Erica Deuel created Spoonful Studios to increase the accessibility of art and arts education to everyone. Using recycled and upcycled materials, Spoonful Studios holds art classes designed to inspire everyone through the creative process. As a non-profit, the studio follows Erica's passion of helping others discover themselves through the art they create.

COMMUNITY DEVELOPMENT — good — EDUCATION & THE ARTS

Spoonful of Imagination

The Spoonful of Imagination Art Studio was a dream that began in February 2016. Experienced artist, crafter, and teacher Erica Deuel had been contemplating opening a retail store to sell some of her creations. The problem was, she never truly enjoyed creating "on demand" to sell items. Deuel got most excited when she helped others to create. For over twelve years, she'd been (and still is) blogging DIY Craft Tutorials for thousands of readers at SpoonfulOfImagination.com. She is especially passionate about the inherent beauty of getting our hands messy, away from devices, and connecting with raw supplies. In that moment, she knows we can enjoy the process of creating something we are proud of.

With an active family of her own it was essential that Deuel still enjoy the creating and joy of the process without feeling like she had to operate in a certain way to build a business.

The art studio was birthed one day while driving through her community in Indiana. Her plan was to open a studio that created time and space for people to learn and use their imaginations. Even though she had to pivot during the changes brought on by lockdown, she continues to create craft kits, and art projects that ship all around the country and bring joy to families near and far.

Deuel also creates local community events and is building online courses to lead others in their own creativity. While the methods of creating have changed through the years, the mission and vision have always stayed the same—add a Spoonful of Imagination to your family for a more beautiful life.

As a company that focuses on helping people, Spoonful of Imagination also gives back by helping to educate families, teachers, and artists see the value and potential in everyday items to be used in the creative process. Art doesn't have to be expensive and she's on a mission to help others realize if we focus more on the process of creating, we can use cardboard, cans, bottle caps, nature's creations and so much more to create and keep the cost down. With a little imagination, anything can come to life.

> "Anyone can make a difference, so you don't have to have it be some huge, global campaign... you can start small, and that's just as important."
>
> —BLAKE MYCOSKIE, *founder of Toms Shoes, author, and philanthropist*

111

A business that's fun and helps people?

Every day please—bring the glitter and let's have some fun.

> "Making a meaningful impact that you can maintain requires that you also get to experience it. That's why I suggest staying close to the reason your passion was forged to begin with—by literally seeing, feeling, touching, hearing, tasting, and soaking it all up."
>
> —AMY MCLAREN, *founder of Village Impact, author, and philanthropist*

COMMUNITY DEVELOPMENT

EDUCATION & THE ARTS

Spoonful of Imagination

To learn more about our part in the community that's dedicated to doing good, scan the QR code.

HAPPINESS WILL FOLLOW YOU EVERY WHERE YOU GO. ELVIS
CLOSE YOUR EYES, FA LL IN LOVE, STAY THERE.-RUMI
COURAGE DEAR HEART
C.S. LEWIS
LOVE IS THE WHOLE AND MORE THAN ALL. EE CUMMINGS
KiNDNESS
LOVE
WHAT HAPPENS WHEN PEOPLE OPEN THEIR HEARTS? THEY GET BETTER. HARUKI MURAKAMI
U

This opportunity to build community has been so powerful in bringing less isolation to others, experiencing eye disease of their own. This intentionality provides hope, and that's another thing this brand is all about.

DISCOVER SOMETHING NEW, SOMETHING UNIQUE, SOMETHING... GOOD.

FOUNDATIONAL FUNDING

Two Blind Brothers

When discussing giving back, we often find a personal connection to a particular cause. Often a portion of profits are donated and there is a commitment to making an impact in a particular community of people. Two Blind Brothers is no different, yet the extent of their connection and commitment is greater than some.

Two Blind Brothers launched by Bradford and Bryan Manning donates one hundred percent of their profits to retinal research for eye disease because of their own battle with Stargardt's disease. Stargardt's is a form of juvenile macular degeneration for which there is currently no cure. Bradford and Bryan, diagnosed with this progressive eye disease at just seven years old, are committed to their mission, perhaps in a way that others couldn't be.

Having a family committed to letting them grow up just like other kids in spite of losing their eyesight has become part of the grit that makes this brand work. Instead of getting a pass because something was hard or difficult, they were given a unique perspective—they were lucky. Lucky because they already knew what their challenge was—losing their eyesight.

Two Blind Brothers is a brand that provides luxury casual clothing and gifts. The ultra-soft tee shirts are made from natural fibers and on-point details. But you may wonder why clothing? The brothers share that because their eye disease is progressive, certain activities have become more difficult over time including buying clothes. Stargardt's can also cause color blindness, which is just one more challenge in pairing clothing choices. Once when shopping for clothes, they got separated from each other while trying to find new shirts. When they eventually got back together, they had the same shirt in hand. It took them hours to find it though, and they wanted to give others the chance to make the process easier.

One detail you'll find on each shirt features raised braille accents in puff paint. On the left sleeve is a braille "tag" with the word "feel," a tribute to the mission of Two Blind Brothers: to cure blindness with clothing that focuses on comfort and sense of touch. The shirts also have the color in braille above the bottom right hemline, which allows those with a visual impairment to "read" the color of the shirt. These subtle, yet impactful details are symbolic, functional, and stylish.

By partnering with the Foundation Fighting Blindness, the brothers can dedicate their time to creating an amazing brand while pushing one hundred percent of the profits back to research that is already ongoing. Why one hundred percent? Because they want to donate as much as possible to this important research that can one day lead to a cure. They have also made a commitment to hire blind workers through organizations such as Industries for the Blind in North Carolina to make some of their product line. Providing opportunities for those who have been affected by eye disease is an important part of their mission as well.

And here's the thing. This brand development wouldn't have happened without amazing community support—specifically on social media sites like Facebook. Social media has pushed this brand to new heights through the power of community. Facebook specifically has been an invaluable community platform, and one that's adept at bringing people together and offering a much-needed sense of support. This opportunity to build community has been so powerful in bringing less isolation to others experiencing eye disease of their own. This intentionality provides hope, and that's another thing this brand is all about.

> "A very big passion of mine and that of the people that run our production is finding factories that have fair labor practices and treating them more like partners in our family than people just who are going to produce for us."
>
> —BLAKE MYCOSKIE, *founder of Toms Shoes, author, and philanthropist*

One of the most interesting initiatives that Two Blind Brothers has put together is the Shop Blind program. Offering the opportunity for the average consumer to purchase clothing sight unseen promotes awareness of the obstacles that stand in the way of those afflicted by eye disease. It's a unique concept, with an interesting benefit—aligning yourself empathetically with a community you might not have otherwise interacted with.

With an estimated eleven million people facing retinal eye disease, Two Blind Brothers is a brand that does good in a really big way by raising awareness and donating as much as possible to finding a cure.

To learn more about our part in the community that's dedicated to doing good, scan the QR code.

FOUNDATIONAL FUNDING

Two Blind Brothers

"BETTER COFFEE FOR A BETTER WORLD"

SUPPORTING LOCAL ECONOMIES   **good**   SUSTAINABLE & ETHICAL PRODUCTION

Utopian Coffee

The ongoing story throughout this book revolves among so many of the founders developing a sense of global awareness. Brendon Maxwell is no different than many of our other founders influenced by a global vision and curiosity about the world in general from a very young age. Maxwell's childhood neighbor had lived abroad with his anthropologist parents, and he credits this early interaction with the exposure to global living with fueling his passion for travel. This in turn prompted him to ultimately launch a purpose-driven business in a unique and special way.

From roasting coffee, attending non-profit dinners, and supplying churches with their weekly coffee needs, Brendon's explorations and travels inspired him to do more with

his coffee knowledge and skill. Building a profitable coffee business while still an important goal, the reality of doing the daily work to source beans, roast them, and sell or serve the coffee to customers wasn't the point. In the process of doing this daily work, he recognized the opportunity to do more. Utopian expanded its footprint by also connecting with a wide variety of people, and ultimately helping

> "Giving builds loyal customers and turns those customers into supporters... You can find passion and profit and meaning all at once, right now."
>
> —BLAKE MYCOSKIE, *founder of Toms Shoes, author, and philanthropist*

to provide a more sustainable supply chain to not only be more profitable in business but do good as well.

Of course, as most stories go, growth and expansion often means becoming comfortable with being uncomfortable. Working with family in business sometimes functions really well, and sometimes it doesn't. After years of working together, Maxwell and his cousin realized they needed to go in different directions. Fortunately they were able to do so on good terms. The transition, while difficult, ultimately fueled growth that might not have otherwise occurred without the necessary changes to the existing partnership. Forging forward into new

> "We live at a time in which we have the technology easily to gather information about people thousands of miles away, the ability to significantly influence their lives, and the scientific knowledge to work out what the most effective ways of helping are. For these reasons, few people who have ever existed have had so much power to help others as we have today."
>
> —WILLIAM MACASKILL, *author and philosopher*

territory often means change, but change isn't necessarily wrong or bad. It is often necessary to continue to do good.

Utopian cares not just about serving great coffee. They care deeply about developing long-term partnerships with local farmers all around the world.

These relationships mean elevating the importance of fair wages. Negotiating a fair price for the beans being purchased enables the farmers to pay their workers fairly. These wages impact families, which affect communities, and in turn, an entire country.

This isn't always the case with every other coffee business out there in the marketplace. In fact, there are some ugly truths to be seen about economic exploitation and regulatory bodies that hurt real people. This is why the mission of

Utopian is so important and will make a difference. Helping real people in the entire supply chain will ultimately provide a better end product that everyone will enjoy. Part of that mission has actually helped former cocaine producers convert their farms into coffee production, and honestly, you don't need me to explain why that is better for everyone involved. Strategic partnerships with those born and raised in the countries that are supplying the coffee mean that sustainability in the supply chain will provide long-term relationships with local farmers.

Utopian knows that by focusing on people, they create a product that both does and is good.

To learn more about our part in the community that's dedicated to doing good, scan the QR code.

SUPPORTING LOCAL ECONOMIES

SUSTAINABLE & ETHICAL PRODUCTION

Utopian Coffee

An iconic bag brand that dominates the specialty market with its signature style committed early on to doing good.

FOUNDATIONAL FUNDING | WOMEN'S EMPOWERMENT

Vera Bradley

Co-founders of Vera Bradley, Barbara Bradley Baekgaard and Patricia Miller, began raising funds for breast cancer research in 1993 after losing their dear friend Mary Sloan. Their commitment to this cause raised over 38 million dollars through the last several decades and supported critical advancements in breast cancer research.

Because of this intentional giving campaign and foundational funding, the years of research has led to promising discoveries in diagnosis, treatment, and prevention. Launching the Vera Bradley Foundation for Breast Cancer was a vital step in being able to do more good with focused efforts on finding a cure and improving the quality of life for those affected by this terrible disease. Building on money raised during events, donation drives, and collaborations with special products from Vera Bradley and Pura Vida product lines, the foundation continues to accelerate funding this incredible research year after year.

Vera Bradley has become synonymous in the marketplace with its support for breast cancer research. The entire team at Vera Bradley and so many of their customers remain dedicated to this cause that is near and dear to so many hearts.

Through the years, they've expanded the ways they give back as well. Looking to impact the next generation in a series of collaborations, they provide funding for various children's and women's programs that actively work to better lives in their state and across the nation.

The means to do good often springs from the money that an organization contributes. But Vera Bradley on the other hand has also found ways to contribute with their experience, expertise, and time.

After traveling to the Dominican Republic in 2016, the team recognized an opportunity to help in a different way. Their work with the New Hope Girls (also featured in this book) led to building a safer and more efficient sewing workspace through this important mentorship by Vera Bradley's own makers.

Building sustainability into part of their core initiatives lead to developing an entire product line using recycled materials like plastic bottles. This intentional commitment led to the development of the ReActive line of goods already making a difference in an ongoing trash problem. Each yard of fabric uses sixteen recycled water bottles! Saving more than seven million plastic bottles from going into oceans and landfills, they are just getting started in creating more sustainable design. And here's the thing you'll want to know too—not only are they doing the world more good, but customers are benefiting as well because the styles are lightweight, durable, and water-repellent!

Environmentally conscious consumers value using items that are produced in an intentional and positive way. Increasingly customers prove a dedication to purchasing goods with an added mission.

Additionally, they are working with recycled cotton to add another layer to this focus on sustainability. Using recycled cotton helps fight against water scarcity and global warming making it a better choice.

Beyond these initiatives, encouraging customers to recycle used bags through collaboration with ThredUp is just one more way Vera Bradley stays focused on doing good.

> "It's personal enjoyment that motivates me in everything I do—that, along with a desire to make people happy. Giving others a reason to smile drives all of my interactions, and also the direction of the Vera Bradley brand."
>
> —BARBARA BRADLEY BAEKGAARD, *co-founder of Vera Bradley, author, and philanthropist*

Measuring the impact of their effect on the global supply chain, they remain committed to being a responsible corporate citizen throughout the world.

Vera Bradley reminds us all that the meaning of doing good continually grows and expands. And giving can include a variety of means, including our resources such as our money, our time, and our innovation. Sharing the best members of the team to take on new projects for doing good also reveals another important component that Vera Bradley brings to the table. Do good with excellence. None of the initiatives are done at the end or with leftover time and energy. Rather these are the focus, the forefront of all the rest that follows.

FOUNDATIONAL FUNDING

WOMEN'S EMPOWERMENT

Vera Bradley

To learn more about our part in the community that's dedicated to doing good, scan the QR code.

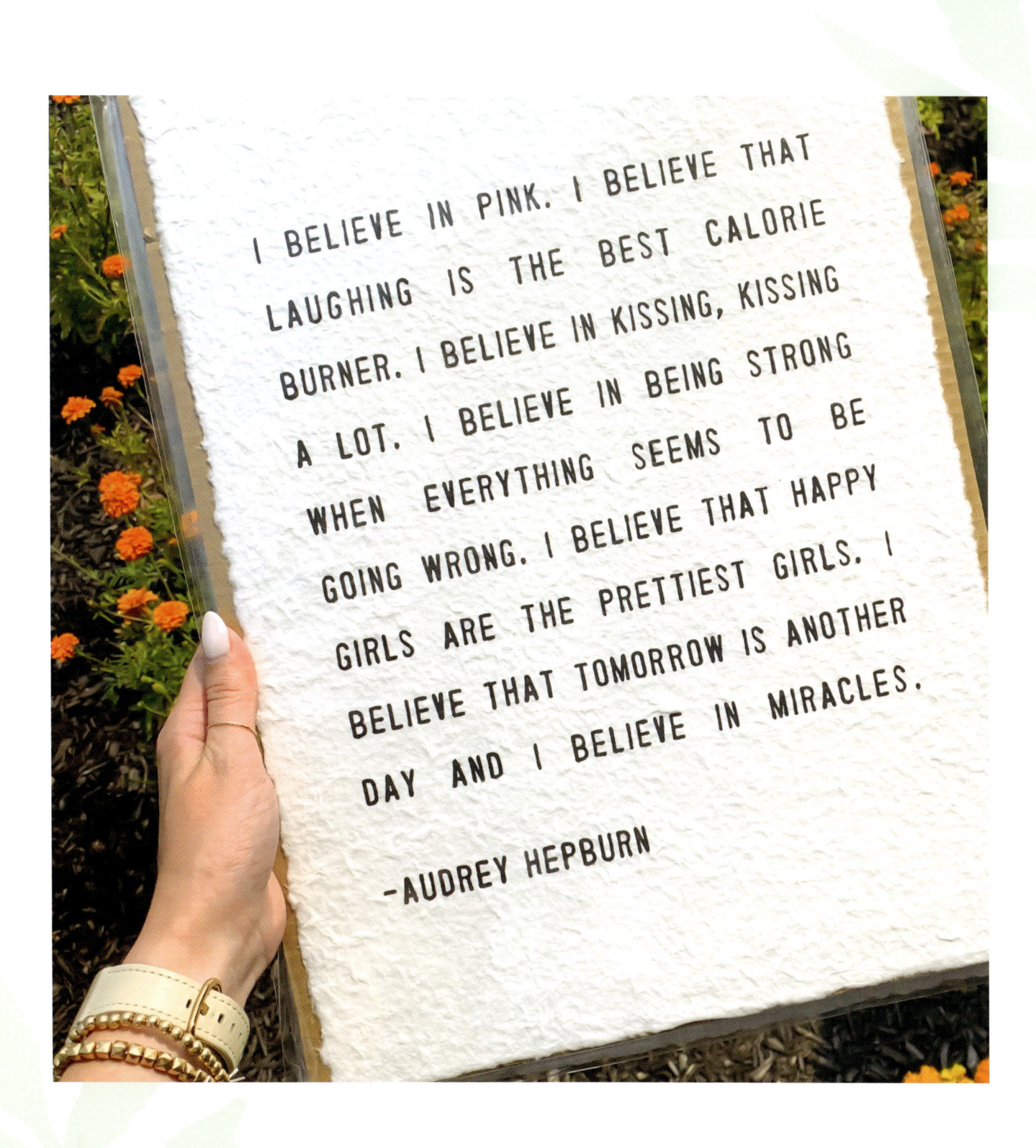

> I believe in pink. I believe that laughing is the best calorie burner. I believe in kissing, kissing a lot. I believe in being strong when everything seems to be going wrong. I believe that happy girls are the prettiest girls. I believe that tomorrow is another day and I believe in miracles.
>
> —Audrey Hepburn

The beauty of Bali and its people is recognized in their craftsmanship and the items being produced are finding their home here in the US today.

goodMRKT is a **connection**, an embrace of shared purpose. This is a **community** where makers and creators embody the challenges of the world and dare to make a difference. Where products with a purpose promote our common bond. goodMRKT is a **collective**, encouraged by a cause and dedicated to doing good. It is a **movement**, inviting you to discover something **new**, something **unique**, something... *good*

WELCOME TO *goodMRKT*

You belong here.

SUPPORTING LOCAL ECONOMIES · good · SUSTAINABLE & ETHICAL PRODUCTION

Village Thrive

Inspiration comes when we least expect it. When doing one thing, a spark of an idea begins our trajectory into a brand-new direction. Suzanne Seick arrived in Bali in 2008 on a humanitarian trip. While there, she realized that the local artisans were creating beautiful, traditional crafts that many people in the United States would love to use in their homes.

Curating a line of these traditional crafts by producing modern home goods products would not only be an incredible business opportunity but would also make an impact among the people she had grown to love by providing a sustainable income for those who lived there. The beauty of Bali and its people is recognized in their craftsmanship and the items being produced are finding their home here in the US today through this seed of an idea launched way back then. As with many of the businesses found amongst these pages, the "and" is the important part. Recognizing the opportunity for a business to

> "We can all use our passions to do more good in the world. And everybody's passion, and everybody's contribution looks completely different."
>
> —AMY MCLAREN, *founder of Village Impact, author, and philanthropist*

also be an intentional way to bring meaningful opportunities and change to others who have a need is a common thread.

Additionally, Seick and her husband Jeremy believe it is not only important to create and curate these beautiful products but to also protect sustainability in Bali. While form and function retain their importance when making beautiful home products, Seick stands firm in the conviction that they must also find a way to use natural materials to create new products. This is a foundational principle for everything Village Thrive does. A variety of materials in the products they sell today include rattan, bamboo, straw, and even pruned coffee branches. Wood, clay, and leather all help round out this diverse and interesting lineup. Creating one-of-a-kind products presents a bit of a challenge. Because these items are made by hand and not by machine, it's a much slower process. But on the other hand, those who are willing to wait for this kind of quality craftsmanship will actually appreciate this part of the individuality and diversity of products. So, the challenge also becomes a positive part of the cycle.

In addition, these types of items must be created by the local artisans in small quantities—to protect the artists, the raw materials, and the local community.

Village Thrive takes regular trips to visit, inspect the production facilities, and talk with the artisans.

The real mission is supporting these local artists to continue being able to do what they love, to elevate their designs by selling more broadly around the world and be able to support their families by this way of life. Being able to do this in an

> "Many things in life just happen, but positive change isn't one of them. Changing anything in our world requires someone to be the catalyst."
>
> —JOHN MAXWELL, *bestselling author, coach, and speaker*

eco-friendly fashion is the cherry on top.

This eco-friendly direction is not just limited to their home products either. This initiative extends outward with eco-friendly packaging and shipping options as well.

Other ways they make a real difference in the lives of the people of Bali once again lie in strategic partnerships. These partnerships mean that they are not launching a new initiative to bring a similar mission to bear but rather are coming alongside existing business, non-profits, and foundations to add financial support to the good work already being done. It's important to note that doing good doesn't always require starting new things. Sometimes it's joining those already in action. With this in mind, Village Thrive has partnered with the The John Fawcett Foundation. This organization brings care to the artisans and people of Bali in the form of eye care. Additionally, Village Thrive is a proud supporter of the Women's Workshop, part of the Bali Life Foundation. Because of the skills taught through the foundation, local mothers earn living wages to provide for their children. Providing jobs for women through Bali Life by purchasing their beautiful macrame goods, women and children can thrive and look forward to a brighter future.

Doing good for the Seicks has meant responding to a need and then setting about to meet that need with diverse methods that are practical and useful.

To learn more about our part in the community that's dedicated to doing good, scan the QR code.

SUPPORTING LOCAL ECONOMIES

SUSTAINABLE & ETHICAL PRODUCTION

Village Thrive

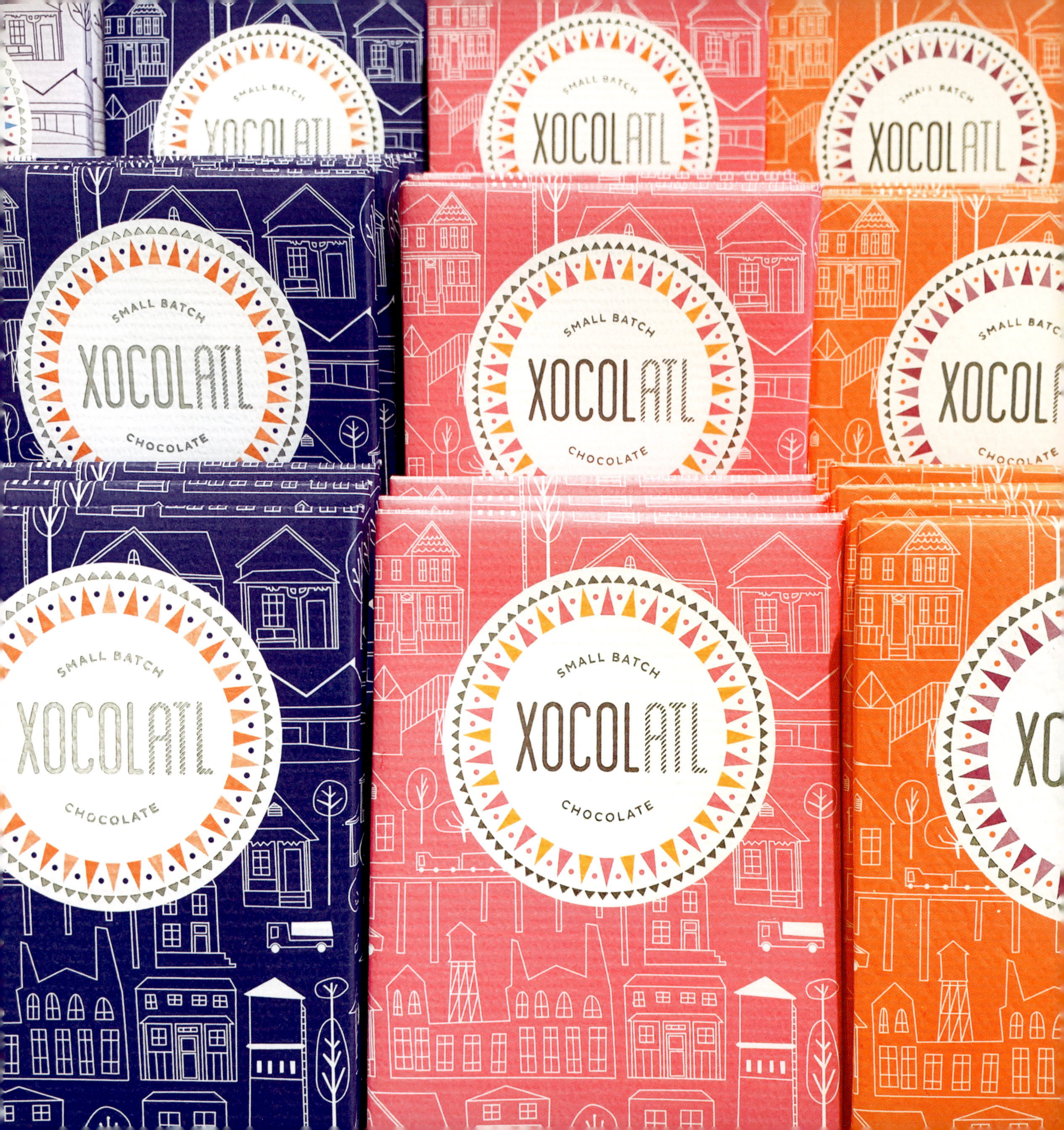
SMALL BATCH
XOCOLATL
CHOCOLATE

SUPPORTING LOCAL ECONOMIES | good | SUSTAINABLE & ETHICAL PRODUCTION

Xocolatl

When they moved to Costa Rica, Elaine Read and Matt Weyandt didn't have a return trip in mind. They were experiencing major burnout in their professional jobs while also caring for a growing family. No longer satisfied with sitting behind a desk while their hearts longed to make real and lasting impact, they made a move that didn't really make sense on paper. Leaving their non-profit humanitarian (Read) and political (Weyandt) jobs, they moved with their three-year-old and five-month old baby in tow to the jungle they had backpacked through just a decade before. An extended season of unemployment meant living on a shoestring budget, but they rented a tiny home and settled in anyway.

What began as a respite and an intentional slow down to their overwhelmed lives in the United States eventually became the turning point in finding a new way to make a difference. After being in the country for just a short time, Read and Weyandt found some familiar routines. They took weekend trips to the market and built relationships with the locals. They made a little room in the budget so they could buy chocolates,

> "We named our company Xocolatl to honor the ancient cultures who first invented chocolate and to connect modern chocolate lovers with its long history in the Americas. And as an Atlanta based company, we just couldn't pass up the ATL in the name!"
> —ELAINE & MATT

which quickly became the highlight of these trips. This chocolate was flavorful, unadulterated, and pure, and they soon discovered that chocolate made from cacao grown on different farms had noticeably different flavors. Over time, they learned that cacao trees thrive in this region because of the forest canopy and proximity to the equator. Unfortunately, because of environmental issues, deforestation to make way for pineapple plantations,

> **WHAT'S IN A NAME?**
> Xocolatl "chock-oh-LAH-tul." The original word for chocolate from the Nahuatl language spoken by Aztecs and Mayans who prepared xocolatl as a sugarless drink made of ground cacao, spices, water, and cornmeal. "Xocol" means bitter and "atl" means water.

and other soil depleting activities, the cacao farmers were struggling.

Most industrial chocolate is made from cacao sourced from Cote d'Ivoire and Ghana—two countries where the cocoa sector is institutionally mired in less-than-fair trade practice. Here Read and Weyandt saw an opportunity. After realizing the quality of the chocolate being produced by the local artisans, a mission developed to help the cacao farmers of Costa Rica really build a sustainable business. The two began learning the skills of making chocolate and aimed to bring this amazing chocolate experience back to their home base in Atlanta.

Becoming a chocolate maker, while not a typical aspiration for most adults today, became an opportunity to make a positive impact on the world. The couple learned the ins and outs of the trade, understanding the need for fair wages and pricing for farmers and chocolate makers. From its simple beginnings, the mission of Xocolatl has evolved with an end goal to benefit the local cacao farmer. This is accomplished by creating sustainability in the supply chain, transparency in the process, and caring for human rights by helping artisans become financially secure.

Returning to Atlanta with Costa Rican cacao, they spent the next year developing recipes, refining techniques, and reaching out to source raw cacao from different origins to highlight the diversity of flavors in cacao. By late 2014, it was time to open a small micro-factory and retail store at the Krog Street Market. They quickly became Atlanta's bean-to-bar craft chocolate company.

While this location gave them a chance to practice and grow their budding chocolate business, it also helped them provide more business to farmers in Costa Rica, Peru, Nicaragua, Tanzania and Uganda—the countries they currently source raw cacao from. Paying above fair-trade pricing to give livable wages to the farmers and the workers doesn't exactly drive higher profits.

Neither does providing their US-based employees healthcare coverage, paid time off, and for an added challenge a desire to become completely carbon neutral. And yet that's just what this mission driven business is doing because Read and Weyandt believe it's the right thing to do.

While they've grown their business and made a difference by doing good, they've discovered another passion—education and support for other chocolatiers. In their own process of elevating the craft of making chocolate, they also seek to educate the marketplace about their choices in sourcing their ingredients, and what they've learned in business so far. This process of giving back to other entrepreneurs in this sector has become so much more than they ever realized it could or would be.

Where do they go from here? Continue doing what they already have been by scaling their businesses. This definitely involves educating and elevating others to work together to accomplish these lofty ideals. I call that a pretty big plan.

> "The purpose of life is a life of purpose."
> —ROBERT BYRNE, *author*

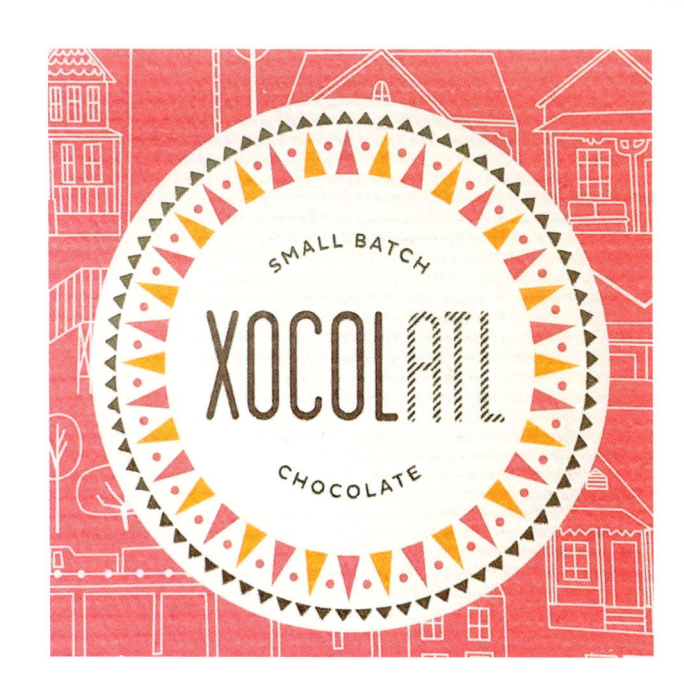

To learn more about our part in the community that's dedicated to doing good, scan the QR code.

SUPPORTING LOCAL ECONOMIES

SUSTAINABLE & ETHICAL PRODUCTION

Xocolatl

SPRING 2021

The product on the shelf is only half the story.

Behind the Story

What happens when a few key business leaders get together to discuss sales and growth strategy within their organization? How do they go from discussing sales and foot traffic for existing storefronts during shutdowns and closures to launching an entirely new store concept and model for doing business altogether? What exactly transpires when creative executives collaborate and develop a tiny idea that snowballs with momentum into something much more than sales and growth strategy?

While no one is sure exactly who launched the initial thread of an idea that is today known as goodMRKT, co-founders Mary Beth Trypus and Harry Cunningham all agree that this collaboration generated a concept they hadn't expected. What began as brainstorming initiatives for retail business during a time of instability became so much more than they had anticipated. And with clear encouragement from Rob Wallstrom, who encouraged the creativity and out of the box thinking necessary for such a maverick entrepreneurial spirit to develop, this granular idea developed quickly into an intentional pursuit of purpose-driven business in an era hungry for doing good.

If our younger generation is teaching us anything it is that they are not content to let the big brands continue to drive business as usual. Instead, they prefer that their dollars are going to causes that are much greater than the latest #OOTD (outfit of the day). Increasingly they are proving their dedication to a more intentionally focused business model than the more cost conscious/discount driven culture of the past. This is part of the core philosophy found within goodMRKT—"something new, something different, something... good"

As this team from iconic brand Vera Bradley considered what a retail shopping experience in their existing stores might look like once we returned to "normal," they recognized a unique opportunity had presented itself. There had never been a better time to do a bit of experimentation. An idea came to the forefront of finding a way to bring more awareness to purpose driven business and the causes behind them.

This was key—identifying businesses built at their core around something more. More than profit potential, more than good people, more than good ideas—rather a *purpose of more*. A business, rather than a nonprofit, whose whole purpose is wrapped up, completely identifying with doing good.

The challenge often lies not with vision in these endeavors rather it lies with execution. Being able to offer beautiful execution of the concept is where the magic happened. Often the idea of doing good is supported by those with good intentions but sloppy handling of details, second-rate design, and even sadder display appeal. In a retail setting, that's enough to kill what might have been a great idea before it even has time to launch. The merchandise selection must work, the display needs to be clean and well-maintained, and the store needs to feel experiential. On

each of these counts, these visionaries brought all of this to the table and more. Having multiple categories of not only products displayed, but stories being told around the store is genius. Utilizing QR codes with consistent branding enables the shopper to learn more about each brand. Snapping a picture of the code links them directly to a video that describes in more detail what the cause is and often directly from the founder themselves. And the causes are as varied as the categories of products. These categories range from apparel and accessories to home and jewelry and the causes cover homelessness to trafficking, and recycling to water for Africa and so much more. The curation of the causes and categories has been expertly researched and executed.

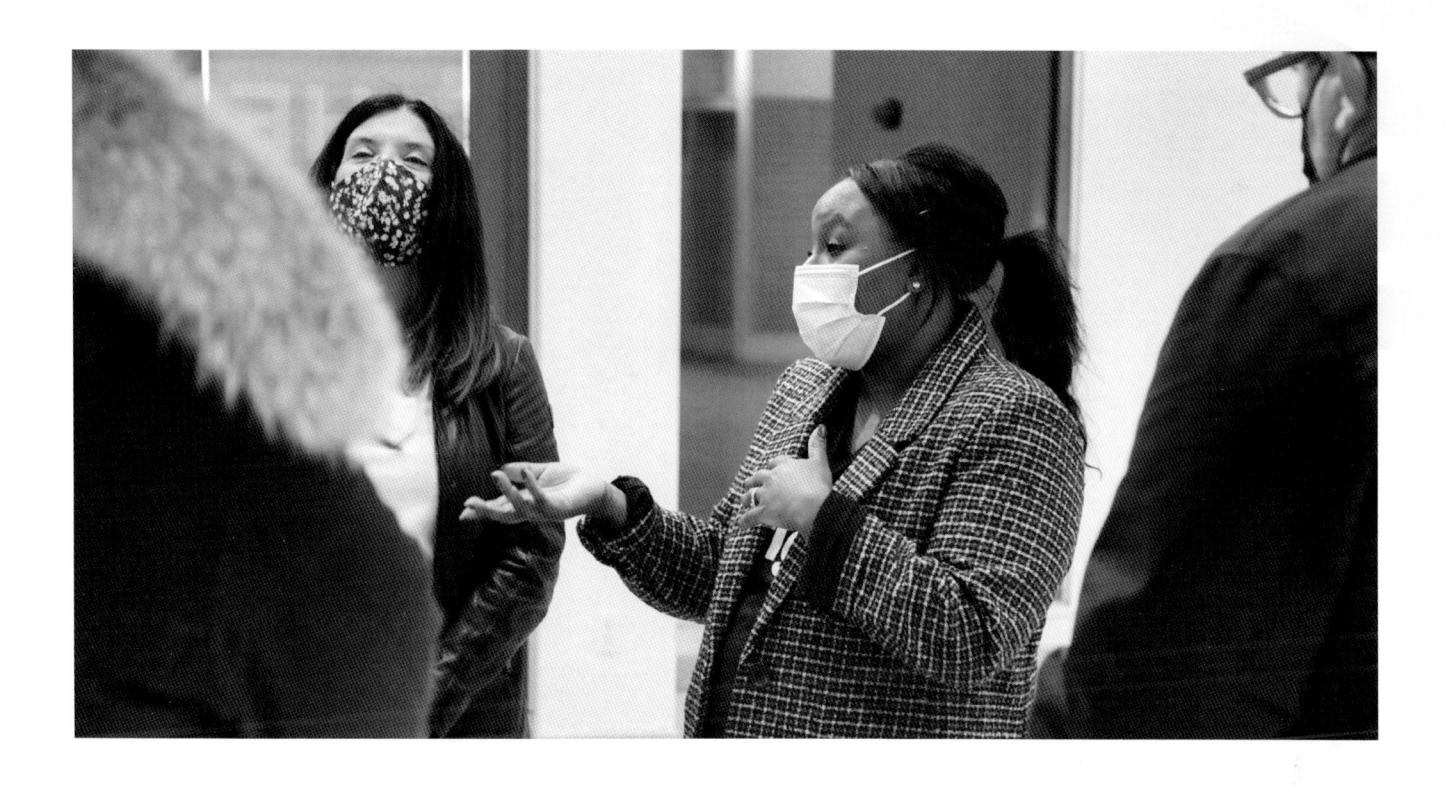

The unifying theme across each brand is the philosophy. Each founder of each brand is dedicated to doing good. This helps to fuel and fulfill the mission of goodMRKT in general—"Good people, great products, exceptional causes."

Not to be missed along the way is the absolutely necessity of a core group with the vision for also coordinating and cultivating the community and collaboration necessary to launch this exciting concept and do it extraordinarily well.

Innovate

Create

Disrupt

Leverage

Synergize

Terms that get thrown around when any entrepreneur works in a new or different way. Some words naturally sound and feel positive, others not so much, but the reality is when launching new ideas there will be a certain amount of disruption. The key is to disrupt in a positive way. And perhaps even more advantageous was the disruption already taking place in the system—in the status quo of business as usual. The ability to leverage this disruption into a positive and to disrupt even further by pursuing business based on doing good makes a tremendous impact and a difference. The impact here is tangible as well because it isn't focused on making us feel good, rather we feel good about literally changing someone's life because of the purchase we make. In this way we are invited to have a part in the story. And this feels good!

The synergy here between the brands is contagious. As the concept grows and matures and the brands each become individually better and more focused, they collectively utilize synergy by becoming greater than the sum of their parts. This force of community created between brands and between consumers built by banding together.

Often collaboration happens accidentally. Someone says, "What do you do?" and remarkably, often that networking conversation brings common goals together. Going to the next level though requires this force that you cannot help but be attracted to within the goodMRKT brand.

Creating that touch point, the focal point of all that is done around the idea of doing good creates a broad consensus and platform to gather around even when the specific mission may vary. This point while broad and general in its scope is also incredibly specific too. *Don't miss this.* This concept was not crafted around BEING good—being someone you are not, being better, being different. That would be such a guilt induced reaction to the information you are presented with. Rather, because it's framed around the idea of doing good, we can each share a part in a story in such a positive and meaningful way. This can look different to different people because doing good can be achieved in a variety of ways. Many times, we think of doing good in grand and noble ways among our community or around the world, yet here there is offered a unique and wonderful alternative. This focal point then becomes so much more—and the opportunity to say—what do I have, what do I do, what can I bring to the table to support your mission and how can we grow together. This is the essence of the Story of Good.

This is the real beauty of goodMRKT. Wallstrom, Cunningham, and Trypus poured themselves into one focused idea and created a new concept that has taken on a life of its own. Walking into an empty space to launch their experiment, they really had no idea what to expect but they had that gut feeling that so many innovators feel deep inside—this will work!

The beauty of this project is also seen in the details and time offered by not only these key ideators in the Vera Bradley family but much more broadly by many who work for the Vera Bradley organization in various roles. So many have volunteered and grown this concept store into the business it is today. So many departments of Vera Bradley's own team from the top down have given their best to put their experience and expertise into creating and executing this vision. In this way their contribution is exponential. In donating of their time, while still working their actual jobs, their physical and mental labors, their knowledge and expertise, they have impacted in a very tangible way not only the existing store and its design, but every single founder that brings their brand to the table. Every single purpose-driven business has been helped by being a part of this collective. Every single volunteer has impacted quite literally thousands of people because of the help provided to each brand.

Here's an important thing to consider as well. In assembling this group of founders with wide ranging experience—brand new entrepreneurs just beginning their journey to long-established brands with years under their belts—not only was there a benefit to the collection and collaboration opportunity in this joint venture, there was also significant expertise to be gained from Cunningham and Trypus and their years of high-level retail experiences. Were they struggling with their IT needs, logistics or supply chain? Did they need a mentor or colleague to bounce ideas off of? Did they need to get an even bigger vision of what they could accomplish? Each of these obstacles could be recognized, reacted to, and resolved.

What these co-founders may not have fully realized was the significance of the vast array of knowledge that they have each accumulated through the years and how much of an impact a word of encouragement, advice, or strategy might move the needle. Helping these businesses grow and succeed by mentoring them and networking them together to support one another in their spaces has built tremendous momentum in the marketplace. And it's only just begun. With more locations being dreamed of in the days ahead and the successful launch of the ecommerce store the sky really is the limit for the potential inside this concept.

Even media night, held before the initial launch in Fort Wayne, Indiana, was handled differently than a regular new business launch might ordinarily offer. Instead of leaving with a swag bag, the media was given no promo items. Why? Because if they give away a mug, someone goes without a week of free water, if they gave away a bib a child was not getting a meal. None of the brands are a giveaway or discount brand because the bottom line isn't dollars and cents instead it's real causes and people that matter.

It's interesting to note though that this notion of doing good isn't suddenly a part of the Vera Bradley mission. Rather it's the natural outflow of a brand that has been at work for years developing initiatives to do good and give back. Barbara Bradley Baekgaard and Patricia Miller, co-founders of this iconic brand, know the importance of collaboration, leadership, and influence. They've committed themselves for years to this ideal of doing good with a long tradition of philanthropy, particularly in raising millions of dollars for breast cancer research.

As goodMRKT continues its journey, the dream also grows. Gathering passionate and inspirational entrepreneurs who support each other improves each brand. The community expands and takes on new challenges while the mission remains in essence the same—doing good. In this way the community creates a broader collective by bringing each customer into the story who dares to make a difference together.

And today we all long for more of that—Community. If we've learned anything these last few years is that we all need each other. And we become very easily dissatisfied with consumerism that is full of ourselves. Less of what makes us happy or comfortable, rather how can we support and benefit others. This mindset will change the world and impact people everywhere. This is just what goodMRKT invites us

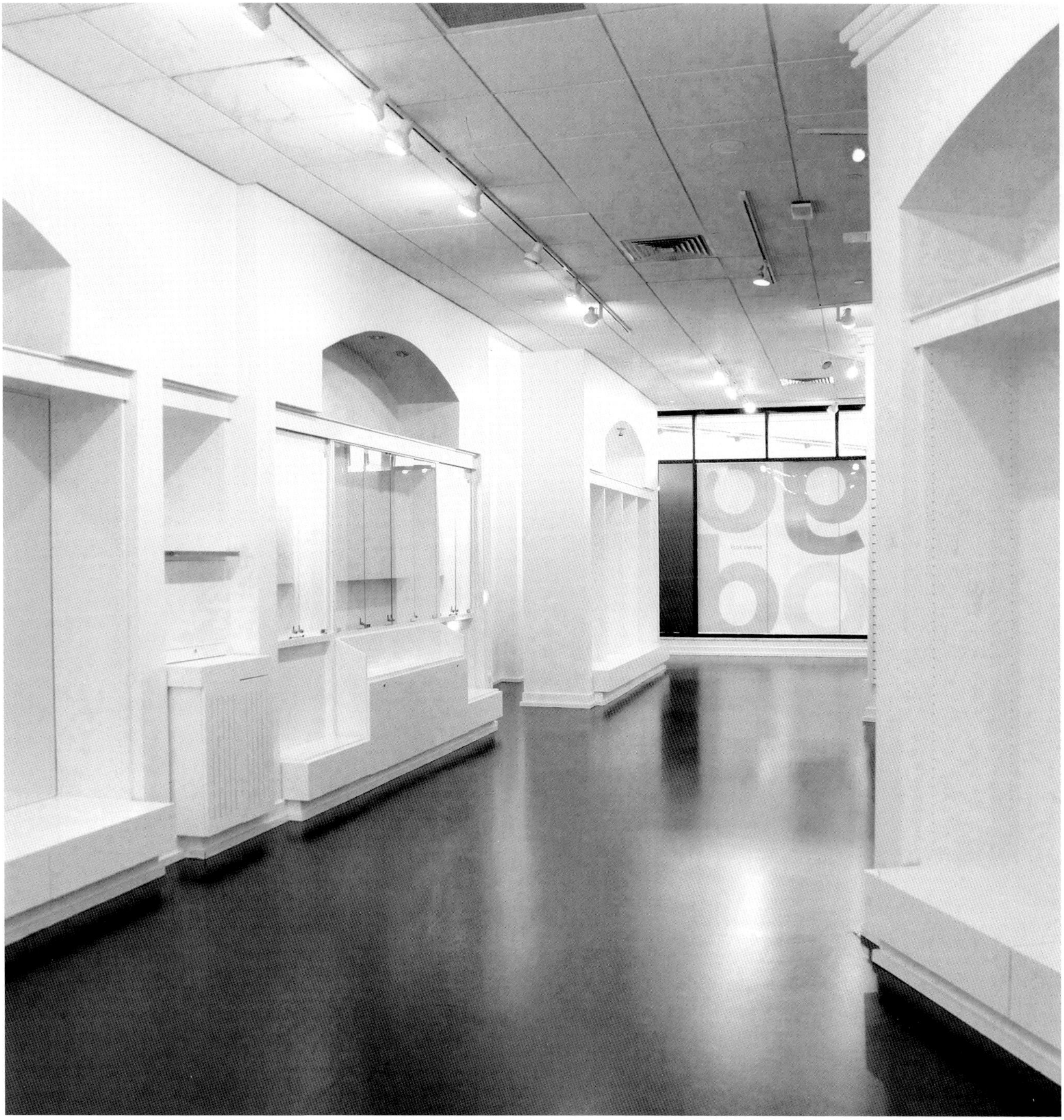

all to do—join the movement. The beautiful thing in joining a movement like this—we can each carry a part and know that in helping others feel a sense of belonging, we also find a place to belong.

Already in just a year's time, this goodMRKT community has helped donate nearly 1,000 blankets to the homeless, supplied over 2,400 gallons of clean water to communities, provided over 1,800 meals for children, and much, much more. And the amazing part of this Story of Good is that they're just getting started!

Don't miss out on this exciting journey—YOU BELONG HERE TOO!

Stay on top of all the latest news and updates from all of the brands featured in this book on our website:

THESTORYOFGOOD.COM

FROM THE AUTHOR

The mantra to purchase with a purpose is incredibly powerful. Recognizing the value in creating purpose around the purchase of any single commodity—whether it's coffee, purses or jewelry—is exponential.

Why exponential? Because everyone needs these commodities at some point.

> Coffee—yes please, on the daily.
>
> Purses—of course, maybe not every size and color but certainly I need a few.
>
> Jewelry—maybe I don't need a new pair of earrings or a bracelet, but I always need small gifts.

And that's why this book and these stories are so special.

If each one of us realized the impact that our purchases have, I truly believe we would conduct business in a different way. I think we would choose different businesses to purchase from, and I believe that we would pursue different endeavors with the realization that we could have an influence in such a positive way.

Because truly it's the easiest thing to do.

Maybe a single purchase of an item is slightly more expensive because it's handcrafted or sourced in another country.

Maybe the item isn't quite your style or interest.

Maybe you've never been affected by a particular obstacle like homelessness, mental illness, or earning a real living wage that so many others face today.

In the end, none of those things matter as we recognize not only the value of doing good with a singular purchase but in the broader sense of uniting people behind a cause or brand and inviting change together.

To me, that would be the greatest good that could occur from the effort to tell these stories well. Yes, please, make a purchase and support these businesses. Indeed, even further become passionate about these causes that are affecting so many people today and need all of us to care. And beyond all this, care enough about people—near and far—to do good to someone in your life even today.

BIBLIOGRAPHY

Arison, Shari. *Activate Your Goodness: Transforming the World Through Doing Good.* Carlsbad: Hay House, 2013.

Baekgaard, Barbara B. *A Colorful Way of Living: How to Be More, Create More, Do More the Vera Bradley Way.* New York: St. Martin's Press, 2017.

"Blake Mycoskie Quotes." BrainyQuote. Accessed November 9, 2022. https://www.brainyquote.com/authors/blake-mycoskie-quotes.

"Doing Good Quotes." BrainyQuote. Accessed November 9, 2022. https://www.brainyquote.com/topics/doing-good-quotes.

"Dorothea Dix Quotes." BrainyQuote. Accessed November 9, 2022. https://www.brainyquote.com/authors/dorothea-dix-quotes.

MacAskill, William. *Doing Good Better: How Effective Altruism Can Help You Help Others, Do Work that Matters, and Make Smarter Choices about Giving Back.* London: Penguin, 2016.

"Martin Luther King, Jr. Quotes." BrainyQuote. Accessed November 9, 2022. https://www.brainyquote.com/quotes/martin_luther_king_jr_137105.

Maxwell, John C., and Rob Hoskins. *Change Your World: How Anyone, Anywhere Can Make a Difference.* 2021.

McLaren, Amy. *Passion to Purpose: A Seven-Step Journey to Shed Self-Doubt, Find Inspiration, and Change Your Life (and the World) for the Better.* Carlsbad: Hay House, 2021.

Mycoskie, Blake. *Start Something That Matters*. New York: Doubleday, 2011.

"A Quote by Edmund Burke." Goodreads | Meet Your Next Favorite Book. Accessed November 9, 2022. https://www.goodreads.com/quotes/90880-nobody-made-a-greater-mistake-than-he-who-did-nothing.

"A Quote by Morgan Harper Nichols." Goodreads | Meet Your Next Favorite Book. Accessed November 9, 2022. https://www.goodreads.com/quotes/9762858-may-you-always-be-the-one-who-notices-the-little.

"Search Results." BrainyQuote. Accessed November 9, 2022. https://www.brainyquote.com/search_results?x=0&y=0&q=purpose+driven+business.

"Shari Arison Quotes." BrainyQuote. Accessed November 9, 2022. https://www.brainyquote.com/authors/shari-arison-quotes.

READ MORE & BE INSPIRED!

ARISON, SHARI.
Activate Your Goodness: Transforming the World Through Doing Good.
Carlsbad: Hay House, 2013.

BAEKGAARD, BARBARA B.
A Colorful Way of Living: How to Be More, Create More, Do More the Vera Bradley Way.
New York: St. Martin's Press, 2017.

MACASKILL, WILLIAM.
Doing Good Better: How Effective Altruism Can Help You Help Others, Do Work that Matters, and Make Smarter Choices about Giving Back.
London: Penguin, 2016.

MAXWELL, JOHN C., AND ROB HOSKINS.
Change Your World: How Anyone, Anywhere Can Make a Difference.
2021.

MCLAREN, AMY.
Passion to Purpose: A Seven-Step Journey to Shed Self-Doubt, Find Inspiration, and Change Your Life (and the World) for the Better.
Carlsbad: Hay House, 2021.

MYCOSKIE, BLAKE.
Start Something That Matters.
New York: Doubleday, 2011.